MW00962419

George Bernard
SHAW
and
Christopher
NEWTON

Explorations of Shavian Theatre

George Bernard
SHAW
and
Christopher
NEWTON

Explorations of Shavian Theatre

by

KEITH GAREBIAN

MOSAIC PRESS

Oakville-New York-London

CANADIAN CATALOGUING IN PUBLICATION DATA

Garebian, Keith, 1943-
    George Bernard Shaw and Christopher Newton: explorations of
Shavian theatre

Includes index.
ISBN 0-88962-508-5

1. Newton, Christopher. 2. Shaw, Bernard, 1856-1950.
3. Shaw Festival (Niagara-on-the-Lake, Ont.).
4. Theatrical producers and directors - Ontario - Niagara-on-the-Lake -
Biography. I. Title.

PN2308.N48G46 1992   792'.0232'092   C92-094783-2

No part of this book may be reproduced or transmitted in any form, by any
means, electronic or mechanical, including photocopying and recording
information storage and retrieval systems, without permission in writing
from the publisher, except by a reviewer who may quote brief passages in
a review.

Published by MOSAIC PRESS, P.O. Box 1032, Oakville, Ontario, L6J
5E9, Canada. Offices and warehouse at 1252 Speers Road, Units #1&2,
Oakville, Ontario, L6L 5N9, Canada.

Mosaic Press acknowledges the assistance of the Canada Council and the
Ontario Arts Council in support of its publishing programme.

Copyright © Keith Garebian, 1993
Design by Patty Gallinger
Typeset by Jackie Ernst
Printed and bound in Canada

ISBN 0-88962-508-5   PB

MOSAIC PRESS:
In Canada:
    MOSAIC PRESS, 1252 Speers Road, Units #1&2, Oakville,
Ontario, L6L 5N9, P.O. Box 1032, Oakville, Ontario, L6J 5E9, Canada.

In the U.K. and Europe by:
    John Calder (Publishers) Ltd., 9-15 Neal St., London, WCZH 9TU,
England

In Loving Memory of my Mother

ACKNOWLEDGEMENTS

I thank the following for their co-operation in the course of this project: Parvin Jahanpour and Nancy Sadek of the Guelph University Theatre Archives; the Metropolitan Toronto Library Theatre Archives; Scott McKowen; B.J. Armstrong; David Cooper; Christopher Donison, Leslie Frankish, Barry MacGregor, Christopher Newton, and Cameron Porteous for interviews; The Society of Authors on behalf of the Bernard Shaw Estate for Permission to use quotations from Shaw; Howard Aster of Mosaic Press; the Ontario Arts Council Writers' Reserve Fund; the CUEW Professional Development Fund of Trent University for a small research and travel grant; and Canadian Actors' Equity and ACTRA for helping me obtain photograph permissions. All reasonable attempts were made to secure such permissions from the numerous performers in the plays under study, and I thank the Shaw Festival for its co-operation in the matter.

CONTENTS

INTRODUCTION

After twelve seasons as leader of the Shaw Festival at Niagara-on-the-Lake, Ontario, Christopher Newton has proved himself to be the most successful artistic director in the country by his critical and commercial successes with a wide repertoire of plays by Shaw and his contemporaries. Nobody who ever saw the Festival productions, during his tenure, of *Heartbreak House, Major Barbara, You Never Can Tell, Man and Superman, Camille, Cavalcade, Cyrano de Bergerac, A Flea in Her Ear, Peter Pan*, or *The Suicide* is likely to forget them. Newton has developed a genuine company of actors, whose effusive praise for his methods and vision is not mere lip-service to the hand that helps feed them. He has shown a remarkable tact and astute shrewdness in his dealings with Boards of Directors, and he has founded The Academy of the Shaw Festival to co-ordinate professional acting classes, skill-exchange programmes, and the annual Shaw Seminar. But his supreme achievement as an artistic director, in an international sense, is his distinctive interpretation of the plays of George Bernard Shaw.

Newton and Shaw. At one time, this pairing would have seemed "not bloody likely," given Newton's professed distaste for a playwright he once viewed as a boring old fogy. He had acted in *Heartbreak House* and *Village Wooing* at the Festival in its very early days, but those experiences merely confirmed his aversion: "Given parts that were too old for me and only minimal direction, I had a terrible time. Frankly the bars in Niagara Falls, NY [*sic*] were far more interesting than those preachy, uninformed performances in the hot sticky Court House.'' (Newton B 313) When he played Charteris in *The Philanderer* in 1980, the year he became artistic director, an old vision returned to him of Shaw's ''unhappy hand, waving a stick, shouting at me over the fence.'' (Newton B 313) It took his own directorial explorations of Shaw to make him change his mind.

Misalliance in the same year suggested the first ''unimagined demons,'' but Newton was still very much in an Edwardian mode. His *Saint Joan* the next year, however, ''wasn't merely an artefact from the twenties washed up on [a] modern beach to be exhibited in a glass case. Here was a play to be handled, felt, experienced with all the senses. These were not rootless ideas floating in a void; these emotions were based on violent feelings.'' (Newton B 313) The design for his 1983 *Caesar and Cleopatra* set a course for him: it made a palpable case for Shavian surrealism, one that all of Newton's subsequent productions (with the obvious exceptions of *On The Rocks* and *Geneva*) have continued to extend.

Newton has established himself as a brilliant Shavian revisionist in the sense that he has avoided mere realism in favour of allegory. Unlike the traditionalists who cannot get beyond their reverence for Shaw's own puritanism, Newton is iconoclastic - at least in terms of his fondness for breaking down the old platitudes about Shaw - the ones which insist that Shaw is a witty pulpiteer or an imp with the mind of a schoolmaster and the unromantic heart of a pamphleteer. Newton destroys such platitudes by his focus on Shaw's radical theatricality. He has remarked to me: ''Shaw is a rebel. Shaw is a surrealist. Shaw is a madman when you dig beneath the surface.''

His production of *Heartbreak House* demonstrated a directorial style that was thoroughly out of the ordinary for this allegory, making the work very much a play of radiant night and dream. His *Major Barbara* kept ironic ambiguities very much alive as it worked out the conflicts within a strong mythological framework. *You Never Can Tell*, usually treated as one of Shaw's trivial entertainments, was done as a colourfully festive play, as serious as it was light-hearted, glittering with almost Shakespearean mirth and wisdom in a harlequinade of free will and the odds against this. His production of *Man and Superman* was clearly the work of one who had a confident vision of Shaw. Renowned Shavian scholar Dan H. Laurence claimed in an address (''The Newton Years At The Shaw Festival 1980-89''): ''...he has made us take a fresh look at Shaw, peeling away the outer layers to enable us to see beneath the frippery the passionate essentials of the work, the repressed sexuality underlying the social conventions of Shaw's day.'' (Laurence 4)

In *The Oxford Companion to Canadian Theatre*, Ronald Bryden gives Newton his due, citing his "liberties with Shaw's plays that directors had long taken with Shakespeare's." (Benson and Conolly 381) Acknowledging that Shavians have complained of Newton's "high-handed ways" with the texts, Bryden also notes that defenders have argued that Newton does "only what a Shaw Festival presumably existed to do - treat Shaw's plays not as period pieces, but as works for all times." The entry goes on to state that Newton has "succeeded in displaying, as seldom before, Shaw's immense powers of theatricality" - one whose spectacular surrealism "makes Shaw seem once more *avant-garde.*" Which is quite a compliment, given the usual approach to Shaw in the English theatre world. Even the great Tyrone Guthrie, one of Newton's exemplars, never got beyond a superficial musicality in Shaw. Guthrie once remarked to Michael Langham: "All you can do with Shaw is to fan the actors out in a semi-circle, put the speaker at the top, and hope for the best." (Rossi 277)

Newton's Shaw is rather over-impulsive at times, warm, and a bit crazy in an Anglo-Irish way. To the open-eyed and open-minded, Newton's Shaw is a revelation. And it is this because it shows a gaiety of mind. A gaiety that is not simply lively or buoyant, but a sportive play of imagination, an interaction of symbol and reality. Newton's Shaw dances with humour as a weapon against neurotic morbidity or corruption.

Part of Newton's success as a Shavian interpreter stems from the fact that he recognizes Shaw's compulsive inconsistency and idiosyncrasy. Margery M. Morgan has written of Shaw's perverse tendency to invert or distort popular Victorian conventions: "A happy inability to treat either his material or his medium with consistent seriousness made him one of the most idiosyncratic of Victorian novelists before ever he wrote for the theatre; Granville Barker drily called him 'a merry fellow' for laughing through his mother's funeral; such jokiness as traditionally afflicts medical and theological students was evident in the remark, 'No flowers, no congratulations,' made on the occasion of his wife's death. Burlesque was a fashion of the day, but it was also expressive of Shaw's personal response to some kinds of experience." (Morgan 2)

Just as Shaw impresses by his differences from his models (Ibsen, Strindberg, Chekhov, Wilde, Shakespeare), Newton impresses by how and where he departs from Shavian theatrical tradition. Newton often employs parody or anti-illusionistic styles in order to highlight Shaw's distortions of reality - distortions which, paradoxically, yield clear insights into characters and situations. Where others see Shaw simply as a jesting Puritan capable of talking good sex without really representing the force on stage, Newton reveals the sexual aggressiveness within the work. In essence, he makes Shaw surprisingly sexy on stage. Where some see Shaw as nothing more than a witty paradoxer with an overrefined moral puritanism, Newton reveals Shaw as a Proteus of the theatre - a mythic figure whose interplay of wit and passion, thought and intuition puts creativity at the service of real life.

In several ways, Newton is himself a set of paradoxes: a middle-class Englishman, turned by himself into a New World adventurer; a humanist with strong Victorian attachments; a propagandist with a most unpedantic style; a clarity-seeker who, nevertheless, likes a sense of danger and ambivalence. All the paradoxes can be traced back to his peculiar past, beginning with his birth in 1936 in a small English village, eventful days at Leeds University, travels in the New World, the first scrambled experiences in professional theatre, and then his career as artistic director, first in Calgary, then in Vancouver, and, climactically, in Niagara-on-the-Lake.

This book is an attempt to show what Christopher Newton has explored in eight of his most significant Shavian productions to date. I have omitted the 1986 *On The Rocks* and the 1988 *Geneva*, first, because neither is one of Shaw's biggest plays, and second, because neither production at the Court House showed Newton's daring Shavian surrealism. *On The Rocks* is a fascinating parable about English politics and the bed-rock of truth. Despite a scene with the Lady in grey robes, a sort of dream-guide who proposes a cure for Sir Arthur Chavender's mental strain, it is wholly rooted in British politics and social manners. Indeed, as critics have noted, not only does it fail to be quite the eerie fantasy it might have been, it also nearly succeeds in eliminating the personal element from the politics. Newton's production, distinguished by a brilliant central performance by Michael Ball, was a successful one of what is essentially a symbolic gesture about revolutionary or repressive violence. (Morgan 285) His production of *Geneva*, on the other hand, was a failure - a grossly shrill caricature, a political debate that was a parody of what was already a burlesque. Instead of achieving a quality of Aristophanic farce, the production attained a tedious, unpleasant comic grimace. But here, at least, Newton had partial dispensation: it was Shaw who had failed with the writing itself, for he had neglected to create a surrealism out of a parable about irrational behaviour.

My book, then, looks to bigger and better things, though it recognizes that not all the other productions were thoroughly successful. But as my impulse is exploratory, descriptive, and impressionistic, this is not a book of rankings or evaluations or a consumer's guide to the theatre. My subject is Shavian production as shaped by Christopher Newton, so the book cuts across both literary and theatre criticism. Its primary purpose is to show what Newton has wrought with works of substantial literary and theatrical merit. So it necessarily filters its commentary through literary and stage lenses. It also presumes a meta-theatrical filter, for in my engagement with Newton and company's interpretation, I have allowed for my own role as a creative collaborator. An extreme version of this approach, as Daniel Leary comments, "is one which sees the play as co-authored by the audience, a view that derives from the insight that if the world is a projection of human consciousness, then the theater is also such a projection," (Leary 2) While I do not subscribe to the extremist version, I do realize that I am a participant in the theatrical effects of Newton's productions. My text *implicitly* asks: What is the meaning? What is the effect? How is the effect achieved? How do the actors, designers, director control the effect? In what ways does the audience become a participant in the effect?

As for the structure of this book, I have begun with a long biographical section on Newton in order to show how his artistic sensibility has been shaped by significant personal and professional experiences. This section will show, I trust, the roots of Newton's own surrealism or heightened sense of perception, feeling, and experience, quite beyond the Edwardian world from which he hailed. I see Christopher Newton the way I view Shaw - as a paradoxer. Newton's Victorian and Edwardian attachments are still seen and felt in his work, but they are always allied to strong modernist tendencies. The biographical chapter shows how Newton was awakened from the innocence of his very English middle-class upbringing and how he has always refused to fit a mould. Attracted by "violent" inconsistency and idiosyncrasy in art, music, and architecture, he has sought to make voyages or journeys that lead to revelations about the spirit of place and culture. This chapter outlines some of the most informative experiences on his sensibility, tracking his development as an artist up to the point where he began to see George Bernard Shaw as an astounding, larger-than-life playwright.

Because Newton stakes much of his Shavian revisionism on an idea of Shaw's surrealism, my second chapter discusses this term and reveals the first palpable signs of surrealism in the 1983 *Caesar and Cleopatra*. Because the surrealism here was shaped principally and almost exclusively by the design, I have not discussed the production as a whole. I have also not provided an academic history or philosophy of surrealism - although I certainly researched these areas - because to have done so would have amounted to an exercise in superfluity. Shaw is certainly not a surrealist in the accepted sense of a Breton, Jarry, Dali, Rimbaud, et cetera. His surrealism is of a special sort - always grounded in realism, but capable of enormous leaps into mystery and quasi-anarchy. However, it is a surrealism that is never quite able to break free from the conventions that have prompted it. My chapter will discuss the paradoxes of this mode, indicating the first clear signs of Newton's expression of Shavian surrealism.

Then my book takes up individual productions in chronological order, providing detailed commentaries on design, acting, and direction. These commentaries show how Newton has progressed as a Shavian director. In the 1980 *Misalliance* he revealed a fairly conservative treatment of the play and failed to magnify the bolder elements of the story. His *Saint Joan* the next year demythicized the story in a starkly austere production which indicated a modernist bias in favour of interpreting the Maid as a mediaeval daredevil rather than as a hallowed saint. He stubbornly defied the purists by eliminating an operatic scale for the speeches, reducing the pageantry to moments of satiric criticism, and stressing the nature of the play as an ensemble-piece. *Heartbreak House* in 1985 demonstrated his growing confidence with a surrealistic dimension. It revealed a fresh vision of this large, intriguing, idiosyncratic work, by reaffirming Shaw's connection with Chekhov, while stressing a dream surrealism. I did not appreciate its subtle brilliance the first time I saw it, but a subsequent viewing forced me to reconsider, and I am pleased to have become a convert. *Major Barbara* in 1987 took a highly developed allegorical path, reducing the centrality of the title-character in favour of new insights into the structural and poetic quality of the play. So assured was his vision of Shaw, that even *You Never Can Tell* - normally written off as a diversionary entertainment - was rediscovered in 1988 for what it really is - an ironic, painful, poignant comic fable about identity and fate. But the best of Newton's achievement was certainly the 1989 *Man and Superman*, in which Shaw's surrealism was expressed in a most potently intriguing manner, and whose psychosexuality should have laid to rest any doubts about Shaw's sexiness on stage. *Misalliance* in 1990 was a problem for me - but not for many others. It seemed to complicate Shaw with diminishing results, though its controlling metaphor was everything that Newton expressly intended. I confess I preferred it on video tape than on stage, perhaps because my own interpretive filters were clogged by the distractions of a large, crowded design. Nevertheless, I recognize the enormous aesthetic arch it described for Newton, and my chapter on it pays homage to this achievement.

The final section of my book is a brief conclusion about Newton's distinguishing characteristics as a Shavian director. It is by no means a complete accounting, for Newton still has fruitful work ahead of him, but it does seek to be a synthesis of his most outstanding features. It is only a decade's summing-up, but it does celebrate his integrity as a director who, while respecting the integrity of a great playwright, seeks fresh theatrical revelations in ways denied to earlier generations. His revisionism is not a self-glorifying exhibition, but a genuine acknowledgement of the genius of Shaw - a genius that invites and hugely rewards new explorations, new revelations, new connections with the modern age.

CHAPTER ONE

A JOURNEY TO SHAW

He was born in a tiny little village that lay between the two small towns of Deal and Sandwich in Kent. Deal was right on the southeast coast, with Sandwich just a little farther inland. Despite their smallness, the towns had significant histories. A municipal borough of Kent, Deal was the reputed landing place of Caesar in 55 B.C. A limb of one of the Cinque Ports, it contained the official residence (Walmer Castle) of the Lord Warden. Sandwich had been one of the great ports during the reigns of Edward II and Henry VII, but then nothing of importance had occurred in it after 1580 once the River Stour silted up. The river had been used for transporting stone for Canterbury Cathedral, and once the river fell out of commercial use, the port shut down to all practical purposes, effectively ending the importance of the town. However, the famous Sir Roger Manwood's School, which had received grants from the town from Elizabethan times to the beginning of the nineteenth century, remained a landmark. It accepted Christopher Newton as one of its very young scholars.

The eldest of three children (he had two sisters), he was expected to become a middle-class wage-earner like his parents - a father who owned gas stations and later sold his business to take up a teaching career, and a mother who was a schoolteacher. Times were difficult. In the war food was scarce, except for what could be grown locally - and rations were the order of the day. "It was a matter of rebuilding," comments Newton.

"It was an extraordinary time. I'd never seen a banana. I didn't know what it was. And I remember seeing ice-cream for the first time after the war. One of the very few memories I have before the war - I must have been two or three - was, in fact, being given an Italian water-ice. I thought the taste was extraordinary. Then there was nothing during the war."

Newton remained at Sir Roger Manwood from the age of eight to eighteen. The school had suffered damage during the war, but as it received no compensation, there had been no renovation. "It was by no means a school that trained statesmen or people who would rule anywhere. I was ultimately trained to be a district officer in the old empire. That's what this school trained for, without specifying this in any way. It didn't help me. It wasn't interested in any boys who were interested in anything that was out of the ordinary. In fact, my interest in music was regarded as weird. So what could they do with me except ask me to deputize in playing the hymn in the morning or something like that." He performed in a few school plays of unusually high quality, and he has fond memories of the role of Mistress Merrythought in *The Knight Of The Burning Pestle*, many of whose lines he can still recite from memory. But music was his first love.

He had learned to play the cello, clarinet, and flute, in addition to the piano, though his repertoire was exceedingly limited by the tastes of his local teachers. "In a sense, pop music *per se* didn't exist in my childhood. The British Broadcasting Corporation didn't encourage popular music. They were pretty *serious* in their efforts to improve the minds of the population. My parents, too, were great encouragers of a serious outlook on life and the arts generally."

The school was very conscious of tradition and manifested the usual English snobbishness towards those who departed from tradition. There was a strict dress code: either gray suits or blue blazers with gray trousers, short trousers till you were twelve, then long trousers, and school cap up to the fifth form, with a straw boater after. It was a very homogenous group, as Newton grew up with sons of local farmers, civil servants, and such. "The most exotic group were the sons of the miners because they were working-class boys rather than middle-class boys. Yet, though the school was snobbish, it offered a liberal education along clearly marked paths. If you elected the army, you went to Sandhurst. If you chose the navy, you took the examinations for Dartmouth. If you aspired to academic excellence, you sat for either Oxford or Cambridge, or - if you were a farmer's son - you could study agriculture at Reading.

Newton refused to fit a mold. He was fascinated by French literature (particularly Anatole France, Stendhal, and Balzac), and though he was always hard-pressed to pass examinations, he feasted on subjects that nobody else was interested in. "I'd suddenly get interested in stuff like South American history or something like that which wasn't taught. I'd get interested because it wasn't taught. It was a Bolshy streak in me - about a mile wide - which turned out to be useful. But at that time, it wasn't. I preferred reading. I must have read practically all of Trollope, a lot of Thackeray, a great deal of Dickens, all of Jane Austen, all the great nineteenth century novelists." It was the age of cheap Penguin classics, so he immersed himself in Herodotus and Apuleius, becoming (he jokes) "a graduate of the Penguin classics school - very useful, very good."

His father was a Yorkshireman who came from south of Leeds, and Newton's favourite teacher had gone to the University of Leeds. So Leeds it was after Sir Roger Manwood's School, commencing one of the most stimulating periods in Newton's life. It was the era of Bonamy Dobrée, Arnold Kettle, G. Wilson Knight, and Norman Jeffares. John E. Stubbs was poet-in-residence. Harold Orton was the Professor of English Language, a Henry Higgins figure who conceived the great dialect atlas of Britain. He could match a student perfectly, by accent or diction, to his place of origin. Some of the faculty would pass as English eccentrics, but they were colourful, highly distinctive, and brilliant.

Bonamy Dobrée would perform a Russian Cossack dance at parties, recite in Basque, and show off his fencing skills. Newton, who had joined a group who published a magazine called *Poetry And Audience*, bumped into him behind the Chemistry Building one day in his first term. "Oh, hello. It's Newton, isn't it? You're the poet, aren't you?" Newton managed shyly: "Well, I have written poetry, Professor Dobrée." "Right, well. This is what you do. You've got three years here. In the first year, make sure you get all these examinations out of the way. The second year is just for you. You can do anything you like. You've just got to pass only one exam at the end, so do anything. You won't get a chance like this again. In the third year, you've got to get a reasonable degree. You needn't get a first. Don't just slave away at the work. The second year, that's yours."

Newton took him at his word, attending the local movie-house that screened European films, racing down to London to take in opera, ballet, and some theatre. There was to be a great awakening for Newton in London, but, for the most part, his days at Leeds were not about the theatre. What was particularly exciting to him in this period was Victorian architecture: "I was at university in a great northern city at a time when people were just re-evaluating Victorian architecture. And I was part of that very young group that went around amazed by this architecture, whereas the group before in their late twenties, thirties, forties, had been brought up to believe that Victorian architecture was ghastly. But I loved it, and to go from my little mediaeval or eighteenth century towns on the southeast coast to this enormous bustling Victorian metropolis of Leeds was somehow a revelation to me. These inventions that were in the air, blackened with smoke but extraordinary to look at, were so wonderful. Leeds Town Hall, for instance, is a famous building by an obscure architect called Cuthbert Broderick....I think there was a violence in Victorian architecture that attracted me. I mean the sense of belief in themselves that they could do anything. Leeds was full of good solid businessmen who commissioned buildings in the Egyptian or Alhambran styles. There was an amazing factory with great glass skylights and the roof itself was sowed as a field. And they kept sheep on the roof. The only problem was that sheep kept bumping into the skylights and falling down into the workrooms.''

Leeds became a fantasy for Newton. ''The canals slipping behind the streets, the thoughts of those amazing railway bridges and viaducts, the idea of trams that still rattled across Woodhouse Moor. You could get a tram which would take you past the university to the Yorkshire cricket grounds or, in the other direction, to a great Elizabethan mansion. It was an extraordinary awakening for me.'' Leeds sharpened his sense of place, alerting him to a magic he had taken for granted as a boy with Welsh connections. His small, enclosed home community had taken its history for granted. He had grown up knowing that Lord Nelson had worshipped in a certain church, or that Queen Elizabeth I had passed through a certain spot, or that the Romans had once built a temple and cellars in a specific region, where it was still possible to find flint arrows.

It was frankly a time of innocence and awakening for him.

Leeds did not shape him for the theatre, however. He acted in mediaeval mystery plays, Shakespeare, Fry, and Eliot, even obtaining the chance to act opposite G. Wilson Knight's Othello. Knight was an actor in the Irving tradition - one of his close friends was Donald Wolfit, king of ham actors - and Knight's Othello, while beautifully spoken, was essentially grand. ''It reminded me more of old style opera than anything else. You didn't come near it as an actor on the stage. It was almost enclosed under a bell-jar. It must have seemed very old-fashioned at the time to people who knew. Everything was considered - every sound, every image. It was thought through. It couldn't have been thought through more completely, and yet the excitement was not in the revelation. I don't remember anything big revealed to me about Othello from Wilson Knight's performance. I learned more from him talking about it than from him doing it.''

But in 1956 he did have his first great theatrical epiphany - Tyrone Guthrie's Old Vic production of *Troilus and Cressida* in Edwardian dress.

Guthrie was then in the *avant-garde* of English Shakespearean directors who treated a play as a musical score, noting its changes of pace, modulations, crescendoes, climaxes, diminuendos. He was more interested, however, in the overall rhythm of a scene rather than in beautiful speaking voices, and, as Anthony Quayle (who worked with him most notably in *Hamlet, Tamburlaine,* and *Henry VIII*) once expressed it, "there were often passages where he didn't care if the audience heard exactly what was said. He aimed for a general impression; the clarity of dialogue was comparatively unimportant. . .He'd throw away twenty lines in order to achieve one which would slam you in the face." (Rossi 19) This deliberate method applied also to his superb choreography, as Quayle revealed in an exquisite analogy: "To a fault he would create busy, swirling scenes in order to achieve the moment of arrested movement, which was then significant. He saw a play, both musically and in movement, as something to be moulded and wielded and made to find its own dynamic rhythm. Sometimes he would impose that rhythm. Sometimes he would half impose and half discover it....It was like a glass-blower who has to blow it and keep it turning so that it is always in movement; because if it gets too thin, it will break, and if it gets too heavy, it will sag." (Rossi 20)

At its best, Guthrie's direction not only made a play a body of living beauty and excitement, it also illuminated the text. For his *Troilus* (which starred John Neville, Paul Rogers, Richard Wordsworth, and a young Tom Kneebone, newly arrived from New Zealand, who played a spear carrier), Guthrie selected an Edwardian style (circa 1912) because he said (as his Pandarus, Paul Rogers, reports) "it was the last moment in history when war was considered as glorious by the young men, when it was as much a sport as grouse shooting, among the better-bred young men - which is why he had the Trojans dressed very much like an Austrian court, with silver cuirasses and lemon yellow uniforms like peacocks, and loving the whole thing." (Rossi 170-171) It was not until the scene with the Myrmidons that the whole thing turned filthy, and the brutal modern aspect of war suddenly raised its head when Achilles murdered Hector. "The thing suddenly turned over and went sour, horrible, disgusting. Until then the chivalry of war was demonstrated, and the Greeks were Prussians in their dress and in their attitude." (Rossi 171)

Newton was excited beyond measure. He found that Guthrie's Edwardian setting made the play crystal clear to modern audiences, and the costuming was so brilliant that the period analogies were illuminated rather than obscured. "Usually Shakespeare was nicely said and it was sung, but it wasn't about anything." Guthrie's production had details that made effective points about the characters and situations. For instance,

Pandarus' remote connection with the royal house of Troy was made in the first scene - the return of the troops from the day's battle - which was done like a scene from Ascot, with Cressida and the servant and Pandarus waving to the troops in high camp. In another scene, the morning after Troilus and Cressida had been to bed together, Pandarus entered with champagne for the lovers. This moment projected the go-between's "motherly" concern for the pair.

Troilus and Cressida did seem capricious to some critics, and it is not even mentioned in James Forsyth's authorized biography of Guthrie (1976), but it appealed strongly to the younger generation of theatre-goers. Kenneth Tynan recalled it fondly in *Curtains* (1961), and J.C. Trewin recognized in this production Guthrie's continuing rebellion against Establishment theatre: "I'm perfectly sure that if it were revived now, that 1956 *Troilus*--capricious though it was--would excite a younger audience just as much as some of the productions by modern young men at Stratford," (Rossi, 38)

Newton was obviously part of the young generation that wanted clarity and excitement. A happy accident had led to this epiphany, for it was that fact of having missed his train back to Leeds that had caused him to visit the Old Vic. "I remember coming out at intermission, going to the bar to buy a beer, and turning around and speaking to somebody. I remember just saying, 'This is wonderful, isn't it?' I don't usually talk to people I haven't been introduced to at intermission. But I had to say something to somebody. And whoever I spoke to recognized I'd had some revelation and didn't downgrade it at all. Thank God!"

The most important thing for him, then, is what excites him, what gives him the *revelation*. A consistently strong pattern in this brief biographical sketch is surely his impulse for new experience, new adventure - not merely *frisson* for its own sake, but stimuli for the imagination and soul, stimuli that do not cause him to lose his *spiritual* innocence, but rather cause this innocence or openness to be sharpened. Newton evidently has the ability to find something strangely beautiful even in the most bizarre dichotomies - as was shown by his fascination with the "violence" of Victorian architecture and the "surrealism" of incongruities at Leeds. He also has an impulse for striking out on his own to new places, new areas of risk and insight, rather like Lord Byron in *Camino Real* who urges: "Make voyages! Attempt them! - there's nothing else...." A part, incidentally, that Newton played at the Vancouver Playhouse.

When his next existential sequence unfolded in the United States - where he did graduate work after his Leeds B.A. - he was charmed by the gracious manners of people in the midwest. "Getting back to innocence,

I found in the States, when I got there in the late fifties, [the amazing] superficial sophistication of America: the beautiful, absolutely exquisite manners of the Americans. I was astonished by it! Small towns in Indiana seemed like a Victorian Arcadia. And the students, I couldn't believe them - jumping out of their cars and opening the doors for their girlfriends. Things like that. The treatment of women was old-fashioned. I hadn't seen anything like this is Britain. We didn't have that. We had manners, but they were different somehow: it was cold, a prescription rather than something innate. The Americans seemed to innately have good manners, and they knew this. And I was just innocent compared with what they knew. They seemed to know about the world. I think my whole education process has been - not about the loss of innocence - but a series of revelations. Like, my God! There's something else here, or another doorway!''

From Henry James to Mark Twain, from Ernest Hemingway to James Baldwin, life is filled with examples of Americans abroad in Europe in quest of ''real'' experience, sophistication, and culture. But here was Newton, from old, historic Deal and Leeds, escaping the conservatism of Britain and seeking revelation in the New World. He wanted to explore America, which was virgin territory to him. ''Chicago I still think of as one of the most romantic places in the world. In the fall when I look out the window here (in Niagara), all I can think of is Chicago, leaves falling and drifting around on the campus at Northwestern. So beautiful, so incredibly sad, and wonderfully romantic.'' He would drive to Chicago to see shows, visit Hannibal, Mississippi, and Montecello, Illinois. ''They were *real* towns. They had barbershops, little courthouses, and corner drugstores where people would go in for raspberry phosphates and stuff like that. Wonderful!''

He left Purdue University where, in addition to doing graduate work and some theatre, he had served as assistant editor of the scholarly journal *Modern Fiction Studies*, and went to the University of Illinois for two years because it was arts-oriented and had a wonderful library. He was still interested in the Victorian novel and half-heartedly started a thesis on Sheridan Le Fanu, Edgar Allan Poe, and the beginning of the horror story. But, as at Leeds, university days were wonderful for him because they were not about little file cards or facts. They were a time of exploration - of people and things and what he could do to give form to his creativity.

Once again his interest in music came to the fore. He had contacts in the music department at Illinois. A friend, Lejaren Hiller, who now teaches at Buffalo, was always one of the most highly regarded of *avant-garde* composers. He was the first man to program a computer to write music. The second was Harry Partch who, it was told, lived in a shack in

Chicago and made his own instruments tuned in quarter tones. This was a time when Newton saw Partch's great work, *The Bewitched*, a strange, compulsive work that featured an enormous marimba eroica and fantastic sequences which involved dancers, singers, and musicians in a deeply American piece. Newton also got to see John Cage and Merce Cunningham, who came for festivals, and in collaboration with Hiller, he wrote the first known electronic score for a stage work (*Cuthbert Bound*). This work had started facetiously. Could one write electronic music as a joke? "But then what happened was that the joke took over and the idea took over, so that it was half on the edge all the time. You could laugh, but you could also be slightly frightened at what was going on in the piece. It was a very interesting exploration for both of us to write this music which was funny but not funny."

This dual tone began to take hold of his imagination in such a compelling way that even today he likes to keep his audiences on edge at a play, so that they are never quite sure when something is merely amusing or not.

It was in Illinois that he took up acting seriously, but his true professional apprenticeship in Canada occurred only after a year's teaching at Bucknell University, Pennsylvania, where he ran the small theatre department. He had ten students for productions in a theatre that seated four hundred. He had taken on the job as a dare to himself, but nearly panicked for he had to teach acting and directing without any real academic or professional experience. The university's system of student-directed plays reduced some of the pressure on him, for he felt that his students knew about as much about directing as he did. At the end of the first season he directed a little Mozart opera, *Bastien and Bastienne*, which he set in a country fair in Iowa at the end of the nineteenth century. This was the first time that he used projections on stage. "I didn't even quite know what projections were. We invented them. We had to make them out of coloured gel to get some sense of light moving through greenery. I wanted a sense of glades, a garden in Cedar Rapids, Iowa, in the 1880s."

Bucknell was a sweet little university, but Newton decided that he couldn't keep on muddling through as Acting Head of the Theatre Department. His frequent trips to New York excited him beyond measure, for he saw outstanding shows such as the Peter Brook *Marat/Sade* and Ethel Merman in *Gypsy*. Never before had he experienced such raw power on stage. The *Marat/Sade* was extraordinary enough, with its atmosphere of mad danger and cruelty and perfect ensemble orchestration. But Merman's natural force, at once demonic and doting, was overwhelming in *Gypsy*. "Couldn't believe it!" Newton still marvels. "Couldn't believe that this person had so much power. I remember moving back in the seat." It was a huge, brassy performance that threatened to knock down all the scenery and anyone within spitting distance.

New York had other charms - including an Old World romance that Newton had so enjoyed about Chicago. "The only modern building was the Seagram's Building, really. Park Avenue was still Park Avenue of the twenties and thirties. So was the rest of the city. It hadn't been rebuilt, so I was able to touch it. I would go to the Upstairs at the Downstairs and sit and listen to Mabel Mercer for the price of a beer. It was lovely knowing some of those old revue artists. I met Thornton Wilder in a bar at the Algonquin. In those days you could get a room at the Algonquin Hotel for as little as $12. And that was true even up to about 1965."

He wanted to become a professional actor but did not know how to audition. He tried to get into the company at the Cleveland Playhouse after they had presented *Volpone* at Bucknell, but failed the audition. Two summers at the Oregon Shakespeare Festival in Ashland - summers that bracketed his year at Bucknell - gave him very good, tough directors. His second summer at Ashland, he travelled to Toronto to audition for Michael Langham and the Stratford Festival, but failed to get accepted. "I was so nervous about all that. He said he didn't want any more Americans. He thought I was American." Newton had a more North American accent that he does now. "I had to. Nobody met a British person in 1957 in the middle of Indiana."

So he ended up in Toronto without any money or job. He went around to the Crest, the CBC and the COC, pretending he was a director, but the powers that were saw through that ruse right away. Fortunately, Tony van Bridge rescued him from his plight with a nervous offer to tour with the Canadian Players. The job offer resulted in a massive release of tension, and with this, a heavy cold. He feared he would be fired. But he survived the cold and played three roles in *Saint Joan*, as well as Cassius in *Julius Caesar*, earning $190 a week, from which he was able to save substantial amounts.

Co-founded by Douglas Campbell and Tom Patterson (with generous financial support from Lady Eaton), the Canadian Players performed from one end of the country to the other for audiences who, for the most part, did not know what they were seeing. "So it was up to us to excite them, *reveal*, do all those things. That's what I found wonderful. That's what it was about for me. And that was a learning experience. How to do that. How to hold the attention of an audience of native people in Lynn Lake. Ken James and I made a pact. He played Titinius and I played Cassius. For both of us it was our first job. The pact was that the audience wouldn't laugh when Cassius committed suicide. And they never did. We were very serious about doing this play, and we wanted to do it well. It was so bizarre. We played in the weirdest places. There were places in the west where you had to run across the ice to get to the other side of the stage which was built on a rink or something. Jack Medley still tells the story of losing a plane when flying up to Lynn Lake. We didn't have lights or scenery. We borrowed whatever lights we could find. We had to build some scenery in the afternoon, then do the show. It was really learning on the job."

The rigours of touring and the excitement of learning on the job offset the dullness of the country. "I was astonished by the size of the country and the dullness. It was terribly dull. It was extremely dull. I remember arriving in Brandon, Manitoba, and there was no book store of any kind. You went to a stationery store and found a shelf or two of books. And I remember buying the *Oxford Book of Canadian Short Stories*, a small pocket version, because I was enthusiastic bout Canada. I wanted to find out what [Canada] was. I wanted to know about it. It was the usual question that I kept asking: Why aren't there any plays? Or where are the books? Where are the short stories? It was a dull country. Most of it was very dull. Toronto was very dull. It didn't seem to have an imaginative reality or a mythic reality. But Toronto was beautiful, and nobody seemed to be noticing that. That was my own secret. Incredibly beautiful. All those ravines and streetcars. You could take the streetcar across the viaduct and you're suddenly floating on green. And parts of the city were breathtaking. The painted houses in Cabbagetown, particularly, and Queen Street West. And the Portuguese areas! All the houses were painted these incredible colours. That was before the Yuppies started sandblasting them."

But Toronto was lonely - particularly if you were an actor. "If you were an actor and out of a job, you couldn't go and take a course. There were no courses at the Maggie Bassett. No way you could practice your craft whatsoever." Newton spent much of this time thumbing through bargain records at Sam the Record Man, until he landed a job at the CBC, playing a journalist, Robin Craven, in the serial *The Other Man*, directed by Eric Till. Douglas Rain played the lead and proved very helpful to Newton. "He's not known as a man who would naturally reach out, because he's so shy. But he was always, from the start, extremely kind to me. I can remember him saying quietly: 'Don't do that' or 'You're overacting. Stop it!'"

Roughly in the same period, Newton befriended John Wood who was working as a radio producer. Newton managed to find new freelance work as an arts program writer for the CBC. Esse Ljungh and Andrew Allan were encouraging writers, but although Newton contributed scripts (particulary one on Jean Cocteau), he wasn't pointed in the right direction.

"I shouldn't necessarily have been writing about Cocteau. I should have been trying to write about Toronto in the twenties. So I'm not sure that anybody believed strongly enough in where they were to encourage other people to explore the world around them. I found that happening later, for instance, in Vancouver in the seventies when I was running the Playhouse there. I couldn't get anybody to write a play which said 'Fuck the French!' - which they were saying in all of the beer parlours in Vancouver. I couldn't get anybody to write that play about the French fact. They wouldn't touch it. They wouldn't touch the reality of what was there."

Newton added to his knowledge of the country by stints at Winnipeg at the Manitoba Theatre Centre (run by John Hirsch), the Shaw Festival (during the joint tenure of Andrew Allan and Sean Mulcahy), and the Vancouver International Festival. In Vancouver he befriended Mike Nichols who was acting opposite him in *Saint Joan* and directing him as Algernon in *The Importance of Being Earnest.* The two became such good friends that Newton was able to sit in on rehearsals of the Broadway production of *Barefoot In The Park*, which propelled Nichols to directorial stardom. He got to know Robert Redford, but he was far more interested in Mildred Natwick because she had been wonderful in Hitchcock's *The Trouble With Harry.* He was also fascinated by the very peculiar Elizabeth Ashley who had been known to hide under bushes in Central Park and throw the production crew into a tizzy. Nichols subsequently asked him to play in the New York production of *The Knack* by Ann Jellicoe. A tonsillitis attack ruined this opportunity, and George Segal acquired the role. But Newton's fortune revived. Brian Bedford, one of the stars, got a film engagement, and Nichols quickly offered Newton his role. He had only a week to prepare, but with Nichols' encouragement and direction, he was able to acquit himself admirably. Because he had a lead in a Broadway show, he was now considered an attractive prospect for the Stratford Festival and was invited by Michael Langham - the very man who had rejected him earlier for being American.

Langham turned out to be one of the most inspiring directors in Newton's career. "His blocking - simply in terms of stage movement - was the greatest I've ever seen in my life. I've never seen anybody who could do what he can do with people moving on the stage. Beautiful, beautiful work. I loved to be directed by him." Unfortunately, Langham's directorial genius was offset by a disturbing attitude in another area. "He was carrying all this colonial baggage with him - not that he wasn't promoting Canadian actors; he was. He was trying to do his best - but he carried with him something that I ran away from....I was born in Britain but was more North American. I brought nothing, no baggage with me. I never studied theatre in England. I never did theatre in England. It was all done here. I'm totally North American from that point of view."

Under Langham, Newton did some good work, particularly as a courtly, self-adoring Orsino in David William's *Twelfth Night*, and as the School Master in Langham's brilliant *The Government Inspector*. Barry MacGregor was also in the Gogol and recalls it as one of the most unforgettable productions he has ever been in, still remembering specific bits of blocking and business nearly a quarter of a century later. Langham had fed Newton with the idea that the School Master had a bladder problem, and Newton, with urine stains down his front, capitalized on this comedy. The crowd scenes were spectacularly choreographed, with every actor thoroughly in character and absolutely real. When a well-known Toronto actor came down to take over a part and started to send up the production, the rest of the cast was horrified and quickly put a stop to this violation of Langham's ensemble method.

The serious creativity was what Newton liked - the fact that total concentration could enrich a performance. The middle dressing-rooms buzzed with the excitement of ensemble-playing, although the younger actors were never quite sure whether the "big boys" were taking the work seriously after they had delivered their big speeches.

There were problems, however, with Langham's regime, and Newton found himself frustrated at times by Langham's tendency to favour "star" actors (such as Christopher Plummer and John Colicos) over lesser lights. There was a distinct pecking order, and Newton belonged to a young group (that included Kenneth Welsh, Heath Lamberts, Neil Munro, Leon Pownall, Neil Dainard, Don Lewis, Al Kozlik, and Briain Petchey), "sort of the gang that supported creatively." This was a period when actors were supposed to have supersized egos, and there were always conflicts breaking out between William Hutt and Leo Ciceri, or between Plummer and the rest. Newton and his gang were "all bored spitless by this carrying-on" and Newton was revulsed by the fact that Plummer could be a *prima donna* and get away with it. Plummer, who had arrived late for the 1967 season and rehearsals for *Antony and Cleopatra*, objected to the business staged by Newton's Pompey in a banquet scene. Newton had already rehearsed a crazed dance with Max Helpmann, substituting for Plummer. However, when Plummer arrived and saw the dance, he stopped and asked Langham scornfully: "Is he going to do this?" Newton was furious: "Yes, I am!"

Plummer always wanted to overpower any rival, and Newton was not sure that Langham ever defended the "little guys" enough. In his own right as the Shaw Festival's artistic director, Newton ensures that ego-conflict does not erupt as scandalously as it did at Stratford. "Of course, I will give in around here to somebody like Bill or Douglas, if it doesn't hurt anyone else. But you don't find that ego anymore, you really don't.

Bill doesn't seem to have it anymore. He's given it up. He doesn't need to bother." During rehearsals for the 1990 *Misalliance*, a friend of Newton looked at the cast list and said: "Oh, that's good. You've just got actors here, not egos!"

What particularly disturbed Newton about Stratford was that the younger members of the company were never made to feel a valued part of the organization, even though senior members such as Hutt, Douglas Rain, and Powys Thomas sometimes went out of their way to make the younger actors feel welcome. But there was something missing. "There was never a real sense of company. That's what I missed. That's what I always wanted. And I think it was from that and from the idea that they turned down some of our suggestions to make it a company that I got turned off."

Langham's successor was Jean Gascon - after a brief period of joint rule by Gascon and John Hirsch, in which time temperamental differences between the two seriously divided the company into factions. Barry MacGregor predicted the failure: "The only thing I've always said about the Hirsch and Gascon thing was that the Board should have been shot, because if you look at history, no way has a Frenchman and a Hungarian ever got on, so why suddenly do you expect this miracle to occur?" Hirsch eventually lost the power struggle, and Gascon took over as sole artistic director. Newton did not fare well with him. "He didn't understand me. He had no idea where I was, what I was about, or what I was trying to do. Later on he seemed quite supportive and friendly, but I didn't get on with him. I didn't like the way he began to run the company. I didn't like the way he treated Hirsch. I don't think he supported Hirsch the way Hirsch needed support. I think Gascon, more than anybody [else], was a bit of a star-fucker. I didn't like it."

Hirsch was more to Newton's liking because Hirsch had ideas and madness in him. "I never saw *The Satyricon*, but I saw other productions of Hirsch's which had a real touch of the genius about them....Hirsch was dangerous, and that's always a bit frightening. Hirsch would dare, he would take daring steps. He was interested in the country, he was interested in the people developing. I liked the way he talked. I liked his ideas. I loved the idea in the *Dream* that the fairies were dirty and filthy, and that when the lovers moved through the woods their clothes were torn off. It was alive. It was vibrant. Hirsch had daring in those days. To take *The Three Musketeers*, this big melodramatic piece and go 'All right, we're doing this full-out, guys.' Langham wouldn't have done that. Langham was more precise."

Nobody - not even Newton himself - would have predicted great things for Christopher Newton, based simply on the Stratford experience.

As an actor he was very diligent and careful, according to Barry MacGregor who, at the time, was not a close friend. But Newton could surprise unexpectedly. As Orsino in *Twelfth Night* he dried on his opening line, while he was being fanned by attendants as he reclined on a couch, attempting to be terribly languorous and fey in a lazy, opulent court. While a lyre provided relaxing music, he struggled to recall: "If music be the food of love, play on." Though quiet and private offstage, with a passion for reading, he did regale a packed audience with an evening reading of *Complete Filth*. The audience listened with delight to Newton, Martha Henry, and Neil Munro, with songs by Nancy Kerr. "It was an evening of total filth," laughs MacGregor, "but it was British filth, so it was all right. If it had [been] Canadian filth, nobody would have gone, or [they] would have disbelieved that there could be such a thing." Newton also directed a small workshop on the main stage, and though the enterprise was excessively modest in scale, it gave him valuable experience with a thrust-stage. "Having done it, I had some sense of shape, yes, but there used to come a point where I stopped and wondered what Langham would do. That usually helped me. And I always tried to use that as a touchstone: what would he have done under those circumstance? Try and recreate his mind. That lasted for some considerable time - must have lasted till about '73 or '74 before I got rid of saying 'What would Langham do now?' I began to vaguely know what to do, or, more importantly, I was able to say: 'I don't know what to do' - which always opens floodgates. Or always somebody else knows what to do, and they'll tell you, and ideas will suddenly start spewing forth."

His real career as director and artistic director began in Calgary in 1967, after Eric Donkin had persuaded him to accept the role of Fancourt Babberley in *Charley's Aunt* at the MAC-14 Club, which had come into being from a 1966 union of two amateur groups, the venerable Workshop 14 and the more *avant-garde* Musicians' and Actors' Club. The appointment of Ken Dyba in 1967 as paid artistic director established the group's semi-professional status, and the first season included *Luv, The Glass Menagerie, Dial 'M' For Murder, Ghosts, The Killing of Sister George, Barefoot In The Park*, and *Charley's Aunt*. Newton had known that Tom Kneebone had just turned down the same job, and he had wanted to stay in Toronto, but Donkin suggested it might be fun to go out west for four or five weeks. At that time Calgary was the last big Canadian city without a professional company, and the next year when MAC-14 decided to become a fully professional company, with Dyba off to England on a Canada Council grant to work as assistant director at the Bristol Old Vic, Newton was asked to take over. "I must have manoeuvred myself into a position where they would ask me. I am a very political person but I'm not actually a manipulative political person. If I see something that I want, I wonder how to get it without hurting anyone. Anyway, I thought this would be lovely to run a company. I[could] do some of the things that Stratford [didn't] seem able to do."

It was Martha Henry who selected the name Theatre Calgary for the company. In those years she was heavily into numerology and during her breaks in the *Dream* at Stratford, she and Newton (who played Oberon to her Titania) would chat in her dressing room. Newton brought her three names for a final selection, and she chose Theatre Calgary because the number of letters in each word was identical - and a lucky seven at that!

Theatre Calgary had no permanent home, but this did not deter Newton who referred to it as "a production unit" composed of "young people with young ideas who work together towards one objective." In the 1968 interview he discussed the theatre's function: "Calgary is a young city. Until quite recently Calgarians were largely concerned about making a *place* to live, with settling in. Now that a considerable number of them have been here for some time, they are more concerned about *how* to live, and it is in this area that I think Theatre Calgary has a real contribution to make...I could put on a series of Broadway successes but I want people to realize that they can get a sense of delight from something quite different," (Stuart 223)

Newton's executive consisted of himself (with responsibility for over-all policy and productions), Richard Dennison as business manager, and diminutive Pat Armstrong as director of public relations. Armstrong was amazing in her energy, drive, commitment, and results. Subscriptions grew by 118 percent in a single year, and by 1969 the theatre had 3,500 subscriptions. Newton engaged the finest talent he could afford - nearly half the Guthrie Award winners from the Stratford Festival, among them James Blendick, Eric Donkin, and Peter Scupham, and others (mainly from Stratford) such as Anne Anglin, Neil Munro, Dana Ivey, Kenneth Welsh, James Edmond, Deborah Kipp, Michael Ball, Frances Hyland, Betty Leighton, and Douglas Campbell. Some actors were extremely generous. Campbell offered to do *The Entertainer* for $200 a week. William Hutt agreed to direct *Gaslight* in exchange for "a bit of money from the Canada Council" and a suite at the Palliser. "He's just wonderful," Newton's comments, "because he acted so grand, and it was very good for us. It gave us credibility. He knew exactly what he was doing. It's about daring. I keep writing down notes to myself: 'Don't stop being daring.' When one stops being daring, that's when one fails in the theatre."

Newton's record at Theatre Calgary was impressive. His theatre sponsored a series of lunch-hour shows, usually readings related to the main-stage plays. An "Actors to the Schools" programme was set up to establish contact with local schools. And workshops in improvisation and basic acting techniques were also created. William Webster was brought in as production stage manager, Kenneth McBane as resident designer, and Joel Miller as Newton's assistant. Newton wrote two musicals - *You Two Stay Here, The Rest Come With Me* (a musical history of Calgary, with music and lyrics by Albertans Allan Rae and Wally Grieve) and the space-rock *Trip* ("The best I can say about that is that it was ahead of its time"). He premièred James Reaney's *The Three Desks*. He revived Dracula ("Nobody revived *Dracula* in those days because it was thought of as a 1920s piece of junk"). He did the first Canadian production of Orton's *Loot*, directed by Elsa Bolem. Frances Hyland directed a good production of Pinter's *The Birthday Party*, and she starred in Strindberg's *The Father*. And Donkin and Kenneth Welsh starred in a "mod" version of *The Alchemist*. All this was superior fare for what was essentially regarded as a regional theatre.

Newton honed his administrative skills on the job. "I've said this before, I've said this to the company here [at the Shaw]: You can't go to the library and take out a book on how to make a great theatre or how to be a good artistic director. There aren't things like that, so you just keep inventing and what you must rely on is what do you want to put on stage."

He managed to stay in control of his board of directors: "I had a tendency in those days just to steamroll the board, actually. If you come up with so many ideas, you know they just can't stop you - if you don't overspend too badly. If you're sensible and don't lose too much money, the board will go along with you. They expect you to come up with ideas. What's terrible is if you get boards where you have people who've got ideas of how theatre should be run. You don't need that. They should be running a theatre or not be there. The board of Theatre Calgary was very good. We were extremely lucky in a man called Fred Scott, Chairman of the Board at the beginning, and then a man called Ted Chapman, who was the president of the local CTV station. He was marvellous. He got us going. He found ways to raise money. He had a TV auction. Nobody had done that before."

The only major crisis Newton faced was in the middle of the 1969-70 season, when the debt-ridden Allied Arts Council dissolved, leaving Newton's theatre suddenly homeless. However, Theatre Calgary was allowed to complete its scheduled season in the Arts Centre, and the crisis passed. Newton resigned as artistic director at the conclusion of the next season. His reason: "I had carried it as far as I had wanted to carry it."

In another two years he was to take over the Vancouver Playhouse after Paxton Whitehead's resignation, and, once again, he set about transforming what was originally a regional theatre into an adventurous, ensemble theatre. His main emphases were on developing an acting company, exploring texts, and establishing an indigenous mythology. He took in every theatrical show he could in the city to discover new talent, and he once used thirty-five actors on stage in a production of *Julius Caesar*, in which a teenaged Nora McLellan (who had impressed him as Lucy in an amateur production of *You're A Good Man, Charlie Brown*) was given a wordless role of Newton's own invention. This *Caesar* almost gave traditionalists conniptions. Designed by Cameron Porteous, it starred Michael Ball as Brutus, Robert Haley as Antony, and Barbara Gordon as Portia. Newton and Porteous collaborated to make it as decadent as Fellini's film version of *The Satyricon*. "It was about something," Newton claims. "It was about the empire. It was about violence on the street. There was one eerie scene where we watched the looters move across this strange, wonderful set that Cameron had given us of just rock. Barbara Gordon as Portia made an entrance which was so electrifying. It was simply that there was a great plinth at the back of the stage with a half-finished mural or mosaic of the head of Caesar. You didn't realize there was a door in it until the entry into the garden. The door opened, and it was backlit. In fact, you thought there was a naked woman standing there because of the backlighting through her dress. [It was] Portia. It was very right because you've got to establish that sexuality."

He lost the old colonial audience of the Playhouse. At the end of his first year, he gathered together his actors and said: "Look! Let's do something with this place. We've got a regional theatre. Let's do something that a regional theatre's never done." He then took the same budget and split it up differently, got a resident company, and put six plays on the main stage. He set up a Young Company to do new work. The main company did pieces such as Shaffer's *Equus*, Shakespeare's *Macbeth*, Buchner's *Leonce and Lena*, and Robert MacDonald's *Camille*. The Young Company - which included Nicola Cavendish, straight out of the University of British Columbia, and Allan Stratton - did works by W.O. Mitchell, Robert Hughes, and Sharon Pollock. Newton also established a theatre in education company, run by Gloria Shapiro Latham, and started the Playhouse Acting School, with Powys Thomas as director. By breaking the mold of regional theatre, he was able to attract increased sponsorship from the Canada Council. "In fact, what we'd done is a beginning version of what we're still doing here - which is European-style theatre."

The main stage production included Derek Goldby's radical version of Molière's *Tartuffe*, starring Heath Lamberts. That was Lamberts' first year at the Playhouse, after he had beseeched Newton one season at

Niagara-on-the-Lake: "Listen, how long is this going to go on that you don't hire me?" When Newton first offered him the title-role of the religious hypocrite, Lamberts remarked: "I can't find a joke in it! And isn't it usually played by tall, thin people?" But Lamberts proved marvellous in the part, in Goldby's dark, violent production.

Another "hit" was Powys Thomas' Lear, which should have been preserved for posterity and would have been, had not the CBC opted, instead, to tape a bad production of a Shakespearean comedy done by a local troupe who had set themselves up in opposition to the Playhouse.

Perhaps Newton's proudest achievement - certainly in terms of an investment in the country's cultural future - was his acting school. He used only three instructors and twelve students - all the latter from the west. He never auditioned east of Winnipeg. Powys Thomas taught acting; his wife Christina taught movement, and Lloy Coutts taught voice. Tuition was kept very low, so budgets were tightly restricted, and it was only because of Powys Thomas' contacts in the profession across Canada that important guest teachers were brought in. Students were permitted into any rehearsal of the main company, and regarded Thomas as their personal mentor. They never did any public performance in the first year, and, in fact, their apprenticeship was kept strictly under wraps, except that Newton alone was allowed to look at their progress in the third month. At the end of their first year they would do a student exercise, for which the main company was the audience. In the second year, however, the approach changed. It was sink or swim! They were thrown right into the Playhouse. But the school was power-packed with the likes of Jim Mezon, Martha Burns, Tom McBeath, Corrine Koslo, Glynis Leyshon, Allan MacInnis, and David Sereda. Unfortunately, Powys Thomas died after that first group's training. Supported by many of his student actors and by Heath Lamberts as the Fool, he had just completed _King Lear_ to great acclaim, gone off to Wales, and suddenly collapsed. Newton was left with a school, a new group of students, and nobody to run things. He turned to Phillip Headley, who had just been appointed to follow Joan Littlewood at Stratford East in London, and at his suggestion, Newton brought in Rodger Hodgman, an Australian who had been teaching in London. This way he was able to have a continuity in policy.

Shortly after, during a performance of Goldby's peculiar _Twelfth Night_ - all smoked glass mirrors and a cast that included Jim Mezon, Nicola Cavendish, Andrew Gillies, and Herb Foster - Newton was sent a note by Calvin Rand and Jack MacKenzie, who had come up from Niagara-on-the-Lake to see the show. What they actually thought of the show or of his Malvolio in _lederhosen_ nobody knows for certain. But they wanted him to take over the Shaw Festival. He declined - and kept refusing their repeated offers, until, enticed by the idea of a bigger company and a bigger mandate than he had so far been used to, he went down to the Shaw to sample the work. What he saw did not particularly appeal to him - except for *Thark* - and he was inclined to turn down the job once again. But upon reflection, he reversed himself, stipulating that Leslie Yeo be invited to run the Festival as a caretaker for a season while he finished up what he was doing at the Playhouse. Newton looked upon Yeo as a reliable old-style actor-manager who could get a show on.

Yeo, in fact, got a few shows on and did more. In an effort to stimulate more revenue, he instituted the lunch-time theatre, the bonus night, and the extra performance on Sunday. Yeo (who had once had his own acting company in England which he then brought to Canada in the fifties) was also able to introduce some fresh actors, making Newton's succession a little easier. However, things were not rosy. After a summer in Romania, Newton arrived to find an enormous deficit of over $700,000. Despite being a good administrator, Yeo had not been able to improve the lackadaisical administration. Newton wanted a big budget, a resident designer, and a permanent repertory company. His vision seemed far too grand for the Shaw Festival which was not yet really past its frippery, anyone-for-tennis approach. His Board did not fully understand what he was talking about, and thought that the Festival already had a company, but they nervously agreed to give him a free hand.

What happened in 1980 caused the Board to have serious misgivings. Preview audiences stormed out of *The Philanderer* and sent angry letters to the press. *Overruled* was dismissed as "overdone Shavian hot air tidbits....at once trivial and leaden." A fifty-one year old Canadian play, *Canuck*, by John Bruce Cowan flopped at the Court House, and Brecht's *A Respectable Wedding* revulsed many spectators. Although Feydeau's *A Flea In Her Ear* was a palpable hit, Radu Penciulescu's version of *The Cherry Orchard* divided critics, with Frank Rich of the *New York Times* complaining that the acting styles ran the gamut from West End farce to Victorian melodrama to Weimar cabaret. As for Newton's own production of *Misalliance*, there were grumblings from Gina Mallet in *The Toronto Star* that the play lacked definition and a proper context, and criticism from Ray Conlogue in *The Globe and Mail* that it was lethargic.

Fulsome barrages of antipathy and floods of vitriol were let loose on Newton the next season. *Saint Joan* brought down the wrath of Shavian purists and theatre critics. The production was termed "shallow," "gimmicky," "mangled." The *Christian Science Monitor* railed: "Nowhere in the production does Mr. Newton give us a sense that he has understood the play. What we have is a stew of traditional (and mostly dull) performances framed in a clichéd avant-gardist [*sic*] theatrical staging." Gina Mallet declared: "After two seasons, and particularly after this season's egregious St Joan [*sic*], in which the maid was projected as a kind of medieval freedom fighter, it is clear that Newton does not have the capacity to be a worthy interpreter of Shaw's plays." Julius Novick of the *Village Voice* thundered: "As for Mr. Newton, the Shaw Festival should either fire him or change its name - or, ideally, hire a co-director who likes and understands Shaw, and leave Mr. Newton free to do what he does well" - which, based on press reaction for that season, meant things such as *Camille*, praised by Novick for its elegance, and hailed by Mallet as "a flamboyantly camp production directed by Newton with a confidence and style never seen in his efforts with GBS."

Many of the criticisms were understandable, but much of Newton's work was often attacked for the wrong reasons. He says in his own defence: "I got attacked for what was essentially work that was from the heart, and was at the heart of what I was doing. The result was that the Board began to lose their faith that they had done the right thing. And certainly some of the stuff that we did in the first year was done on a dare." Nora McLellan once remarked that the company did not expect to last. Newton thinks she was quite right: "We were, in a sense, daring them to say 'Stop that!' Not that one expected them to *say* it, but we were at the same time daring them to. That's why we did *A Respectable Wedding*. Things had to happen. But in order to happen, you have to have a permanent company. You have to have a permanent design department. You have to build these things. They can't happen by just grabbing a few people off the street. It doesn't work like that."

Newton was not finding his audiences. "We didn't necessarily need the audience that had come before. If they wanted to come with us, we would have been very happy, but we needed a new audience. I couldn't stand the productions of Shaw that I had seen here. They were terrible. They were all sung or treated as bad Oscar Wilde. I didn't even like Shaw. I thought he was an old bore." Newton assisted in his own demolition by imperious statements on the limited merits of Shaw, allowing valour to get the better part of discretion. He proclaimed in the press that Shaw is "a good coat hanger for the period, but I don't think he's the greatest playwright. His ideas got a little confined. I'm not sure that Shaw had a new thought after the 1890s."

All his other controversies paled in comparison with the one he started with such careless remarks. He had been virulently attacked for expanding the repertoire of Continental plays and diminishing the number of Shavian ones in a season; he had been hammered for wanting to appropriate part of the Commons for a Pavilion Theatre next to the Festival one; and he and his actors had been reviled for "peacock" vanity. But all these attacks dwindled in significance in relation to his arrogance towards Shaw.

Newton recently noted in a book review of Michael Holroyd's first volume of Shaw's biography: "I didn't care for Shaw's plays, and the man himself haunted my memory as a boring old geezer lecturing everyone from the radio, always knowing better than anyone else what was wrong with everything. He was the kind of uneven-tempered old farmer who would chase one out of his field with a stick." (Newton B 313) And in 1980 he was marching in to the Shaw Festival with little sympathy for a canon he was supposed to be guarding and promoting. His initial attitude was (in his own words) "an obnoxious 'so-show-me-what-all-the-fuss-is-about'" one. (Newton B 313)

But the minute he began to direct Shaw, he realized the fatuousness of his own attitude. "I knew that there was more to Shaw than I had ever dreamed of: surreal, resonant, troubling. A look beneath the surface and I glimpsed unimagined demons." It was a revelation, from which he has developed an utter conviction in Shaw's greatness as a playwright. "If you take the plays seriously and see them as profound plays, then they are profound plays. Before I started directing Shaw, I always thought he was what I'd always seen him presented as - as some kind of drawing-room comedian who didn't work anymore. No! *Misalliance* is about a forest in which lovers move and get lost. *Heartbreak House* is a magical strange house. In *You Never Can Tell* they're at the seaside, and the seaside is full of delight - seabathing and sunshine let into rooms and craziness, delight, happiness."

What has particularly inspired Newton's ever-growing fascination with Shaw is not the playwright's ideas as much as the passions and heightened sense of reality. Newton persists in calling Shaw a surrealist, and it is here that we should pause to understand the postulates behind this vision of one who is usually regarded as anything but a surrealist! But Newton charms audiences to see Shaw with new eyes. He compels them to discard certain hoary platitudes and to accept the truth that there are "demons" in the plays, violent feelings about love and life, paradoxes about dream and consciousness, a crazy freedom, and transcendental leaps of imagination.

CHAPTER TWO

SHAVIAN SURREALISM

Newton believes that Shaw might have been a magic realist if he were to be writing now. "Things that seem crazy intrude upon the world that he creates. He creates a world that goes beyond the realistic....It's very deep and large and it's why I call him a surrealist. He sees that what on the surface could be regarded as ordinary life is, in fact, magical - that what seems to be one thing can often turn out to be another....It's as if the world is constructed or made up of a whole series of individually understandable events, but which put together make something which is very difficult to get ahold of....It's not naturalistic theatre. The reasoning behind it - the reasoning why things are happening - is not at all linear. It's something else. Something else is going on. And you have to keep asking 'why?'"

Why doesn't Newton stop at calling Shaw's theatre symbolic or allegorical? "Because that doesn't cover all the elements in it - the fact that you can take a play, for instance, like *Heartbreak House* which at the end of the first act breaks into poetry. Just the simple strangeness - the idea of ending the play with [Randall's] flute, the fact of a bomb going off. In fact, you don't even know in the play whether there is a war going on - which is understandable. If there is a war going on, people don't often talk about it. You're never quite sure if it is actually happening. I think by calling him a surrealist it somehow pulls together all these disparate elements that I find in it. Because surrealism for me is larger than realism, and it's that which intrigues me about him - or one of the things that intrigues me."

Newton begins with a sense of Shaw's heightened reality and then notes how the playwright leaps even beyond that. "And one mustn't be afraid of these leaps; they're grounded. In the great plays, they're absolutely grounded in something real, and it's through the understanding of the real that you find where these leaps are taking it all and what they're about. Take what seems like, in one way, a simplistic play in terms of pure shape - *Man and Superman*, without the Don Juan in Hell sequence. There are still elements in it which, in many ways, are completely crazy. Taking off across Europe in a fast car - completely mad. It's not just wealthy people at play. There's something larger going on here, and ending up in Spain with visits to the Alhambra. What is all this? I mean, this is extraordinary. They're not just taking off for Brighton. It's somewhere in Spain, something dry, something which is magical in a different way, a place where passions are heightened."

Although far from precise in his explanations, Newton does convey ideas with which to explore the nature and scope of Shaw's surrealism. Behind his struggle to clarify his own concept is a real sense of Shaw's largeness as a playwright of mysterious essences. Words and phrases such as "magic," "crazy," "simple strangeness," "leaps," "passions being heightened" all coalesce around the image of Shaw as something other than a pedantic wit or a salon satirist. And although the term "surrealist" at first seems grossly at odds with the critical consensus of Shaw as a moralist, it is not a radical impertinence for Newton to apply it.

It is generally acknowledged that, technically, Shaw's plays are not revolutionary in terms of stagecraft. Shaw remained candid about his debt to old theatrical forms and inspirations:

> Opera taught me to shape my plays into recitatives, arias, duets, trios, ensemble finales, and bravura pieces to display the technical accomplishments of the executants, with the quaint result that all the critics, friendly and hostile, took my plays to be so new, so extraordinary, so revolutionary, that the Times critic declared they were not plays at all as plays had been defined for all time by Aristotle. The trust was that I was going back atavistically to Aristotle, to the tribune stage, to the circus, to the didactic Mysteries, to the word music of Shakespear, to the forms of my idol Mozart, and to the stage business of the great players whom I had actually seen acting, from Barry Sullivan, Salvini, and Ristori to Coquelin and Chaliapin. I was, and still am, the most old-fashioned playwright outside China and Japan. (West 294)

And yet he was possibly overstating the case. True, his early plays - especially those collected in *Plays Unpleasant* - were primarily didactic and propagandistic, and conservative in form, despite certain pressures to shock his audiences. He wanted the dramatic and comic power of the plays "to force the spectator to face unpleasant facts." (Shaw I 25) But even as he wrote such plays to deal with social evils, he allowed for a dynamic of less precise, definite, or rational conflicts. As Margery Morgan has shown in *The Shavian Playground*, the *Plays Unpleasant* have some quite unexpected delights, despite the rather obvious rough patches, unfinished characterization, and inadequate dramatic rhythms. The "real originality" of *Widowers' Houses*, for instance, is the tension between "socialist logic and private emotion." (Morgan 24) Blanche Sartorius does not have the good humour or charm of a Saint Joan or Ellie Dunn or Ann Whitefield. But her violent passion is almost like a *possession*. The symbolic setting of the Ibsen Club in *The Philanderer* is but a hint of the aggressive and subversive nature of this play. "We are the dramatist's victims, tormented not merely by the questioning of our opinions but by a gratuitous operation on the possibly diseased emotions which attach us to our moral values." (Morgan 33) As for *Mrs. Warren's Profession*, "Shaw exploits the impossible character of farce to subvert normally accepted values and suspend the mechanism of inhibition." (Morgan 37) Melodrama and farce are strong and plentiful, yet there are shocks in Vivie's "self-directed violence" (Morgan 41) and in the routing of customary morality by *instinct*. (Morgan 38) The dramatic disappointment of the final confrontation between Kitty Warren and her daughter derives from Shaw's "misjudgment of the nature of what he had to portray," (Morgan 44) but there is an inescapable sense of his temptation - resisted but residualized -to reach a tragic closure.

Shaw's plays often have elements of what Morgan calls the "stage exotic." *Caesar and Cleopatra* can be seen as an entertainment for adult children. Robin Phillips, in fact, once set a 1971 production for the Chichester Festival in an all-white nursery, replete with cut-out wooden rocking horse and a rag doll for the Queen. *Geneva* is a merry charade. *Saint Joan* uses many conventions of English pantomime. And *Arms and the Man* gives us a metaphor of war, rather than the reality of it. Certainly, Shavian innocence pales beside William Blake's radiant subconscious forces in his poems of innocence, but in Shaw, as in Blake, there are links between innocence and anarchic undertows of sexual freedom. Even so early a play as *Candida* has *leitmotifs* of a sexual Life Force. Candida's "seductive blandness" (Morgan 80) serves as a check on the comedy and ecstasy of Marchbanks, Burgess, and the revellers from a champagne supper. She is the moral inhibitor, but Shaw is aware of this and allows for a fascinating tension between her Virgin Mother image and the Dionysian strains of Marchbanks.

It can already be sensed that Shaw was not a simple realist. By mid-career he was disavowing himself as a representationalist or realist. In a reply to Alexander Bakshy's analysis of his plays in *The Theatre Unbound*, Shaw discussed his theories of craftsmanship:

> You will understand that my plays are not constructed plays: they grow naturally. If you 'construct' a play: that is, if you plan your play beforehand, and then carry out your plan, you will find yourself in the position of a person putting together a jig-saw puzzle, absorbed and intensely interested in an operation which, to a spectator, is unbearably dull. The scenes must be born alive. If they are not new to you as you write, and sometimes quite contrary to the expectations with which you have begun them, they are dead wood.
>
> A live play constructs itself with a subtlety, and often with a mechanical ingenuity, that often deludes critics into holding the author up as the most crafty of artificers when he has never, in writing his play, known what one of his characters would say until another character gave the cue. (West 184)

In rejecting what he called "stage life" in favour of "real life," Shaw was not simply plumping for a reproduction of the quotidian, banal, common light of common day:

> Stage life is *artificially* simple and well understood by the masses but it is very *stale*; its feeling is *conventional*; it is totally *unsuggestive of thought* because all its *conclusions are foregone*; and it is constantly in conflict with the real knowledge which the separate members of the audience derive from their own daily occupations. For instance, a naval or military melodrama only goes down with civilians. Real life, on the other hand, is so ill understood, even by its clearest observers, that no sort of consistency is discoverable in it; there is no 'natural justice' corresponding to that simple and pleasant concept, 'poetic justice'; and, as a whole, it is unthinkable. But, on the other hand, it is *credible, stimulating, suggestive, various, free from creeds and systems* - in short, it is real. (West 20) (italics mine)

It should be evident from the above that Shaw's concept of realism incorporated several of the basic elements of surrealism. His concept was of a new mode of perception that was aimed at transforming life. In advocating a theatre that, like real life, was "various" and "free from creeds and systems," Shaw was resisting concepts of control, condensation, and rules - those very elements so markedly characteristic of classicist literature. The surrealist movement (promoted by Breton, Jarry, Apollinaire, Rimbaud, Magritte, Ernst, Dali, et cetera) was opposed to anything against the emancipation of spirit, (Matthews 169) and all its fundamental impulses towards the primacy of imagination, dream, automatic writing, and anarchic laughter were illustrations of creative expectancy, a regenerative transformation of the world by a mediation between man and the marvellous. Shaw, like the surrealists, wanted the emancipation of spirit and more of the marvellous in quotidian life.

But does not Shaw's scrupulous and often pontifical didacticism disqualify him from surrealism? No, for as Wallace Fowlie argues: "There is a pedantic side to surrealism, an overemphasis on the exclusive use of the automatic method of producing a work of art, which has prevented its fullest development." (Fowlie 175) Ironically, of course, Shaw's pedantry did not issue from either an emphasis or overemphasis of automatic writing; instead it issued from his moral and intellectual convictions that he was determined to express in effective forms. If there was any element of the automatic in Shaw, it was in his witty paradox. But this was automatic in a rhetorical sense, and not as a subconscious phenomenon. Shaw was too keen a thinker to surrender himself *completely* to fantasy or hallucination. His plays were certainly marked by control, choice, and synthesis - elements of classicism - yet they also manifested far less order and synthesis than is usually thought - as can be seen in the overall form of *Misalliance* or in the endings of *Major Barbara, You Never Can Tell*, and *Heartbreak House*. Shaw professed not be governed by principles, and in a letter to *The New York Times* on June 2, 1912, he set out his meaning:

> I am not governed by principles; I am inspired, how or why I cannot explain, because I do not know; but inspiration it must be; for it comes to me without any reference to my own ends or interest.

> I find myself possessed of a theme in the following manner. I am pushed by a natural need to set to work to write down the conversations that come into my head unaccountably. At first I hardly know the speakers, and cannot find names for them. They become more and more familiar, and I learn their names. Finally I come to know them very well, and discover what it is they are driving at, and why they have said and done the things I have been moved to set down.

>   This is not being 'guided by principles'; it is
> hallucination; and sane hallucination is what we call play or
> drama. I do not select my methods: they are imposed upon
> me by a hundred considerations: by the physical
> considerations of theatrical representation, by the laws
> devised by the municipality to guard against fires and other
> accidents to which theatres are liable, by the economics of
> theatrical commerce, by the nature and limits of the art of
> acting, by the capacity of the spectators for understanding
> what they see and hear, and by the accidental circumstances
> of the particular production in hand. (West 116-117)

The key phrases here would suggest an appreciable degree of
spontaneity in his writing.

In "My Way With a Play," printed in *The Observer* (September 29,
1946), he claimed to be "furiously opposed" to the method and principles
of "fashionable London theatre" - the theatre of Pinero, Jones, Carton,
Grundy, and Wilde:

> They were all for 'constructed' plays, the technique of
> construction being that made fashionable by Scribe in Paris,
> and the sanction claimed for it no less than that of Aristotle.
> Plays manufactured on this plan, and called 'well-made
> plays,' I compared derisively to cats'-cradles, clockwork
> mice, mechanical rabbits, and the like. The critics reported
> that my plays were not plays, whatever other entertainment
> value they might possess.
>   Thus, instead of taking a step forward technically in
> the order of the calendar, I threw off Paris and went back to
> Shakespear, to the Bible, to Bunyan, Walter Scott, Dickens,
> and Dumas *père*, Mozart, and Verdi, in whom I had been
> soaked from my childhood. Instead of planning my plays I
> let them grow as they came, and hardly ever wrote a page
> foreknowing what the next page would be. When I tried a
> plot I found that it substituted the absorbing interest of
> putting it together like a jig-saw puzzle (the dullest of all
> occupations for the lookers-on) for communicable dramatic
> interest, loading the story with deadwood and spoiling it, as
> in the lamentable case of Goldsmitih's Good Natur'd Man,
> which without its plot would have been a classic. (West 268)

Besides claiming that he was, in fact, quite traditional in his
emphasis on the art of story-telling as practised by all great writers and

opera-composers, Shaw was here also making a claim for organic rather than mechanical structure - or, to put it differently, he was advancing his own mode of imaginative organization.

Elsewhere, Shaw contended that his plays were not "constructed" in the usual sense of the word, and he went on to hold that he was not a Rationalist:

> I am not a Rationalist. I began, as everybody did in the nineteenth century, by writing novels. I wrote two (1879 and 1880) within Rationalist limits; and the hero of the second was a thorough Rationalist. I then discovered that Rationalism was an impasse, and that I could not get a step further with it. In my third novel I threw it over completely: my hero was a sort of Beethoven. By the time I began writing plays I had left Rationalism far behind me; what was mistaken for it in my plays was a very vigorous exercise of a power of reasoning which I had cultivated as a sociologist and economist. I could therefore reason on problems from which most writers of fiction took refuge in mushy emotionalism. (West 184)

Was Shaw merely being an impish trickster once again in deliberately misleading his readers? Not so. He was eager, it seems to me, to impress on his public the crucial distinction between reason as a philosophical tool and reasoning as an essential passion: "...not for a moment will you find in my plays any assumption that reason is more than an instrument. What you will find, however, is the belief that intellect is essentially a passion, and that the search for enlightenment of any sort is far more interesting and enduring than, say, the sexual pursuit of a woman by a man, which was the only interest the plays of my early days regarded as proper to the theatre: a play without it was 'not a play.'" (West 184-185)

In some ways, Shaw appeared to contradict himself on his craft. While resisting the labels of "representationalist" or "realist," he, nevertheless, believed that his plays showed real life rather than stage life. While denouncing the artifices of the mechanically "well-made" play, he insisted that his craft rose from Victorian stock-company theatre. And while insisting that he was not a Rationalist, he boasted that he reasoned out every sentence to the utmost of his capacity before committing it to print.

The paradoxes of his apologies for craft highlight the paradoxes of his surrealism. For Shaw almost every statement had its counter-statement, and, so, when we look for surrealistic elements and tensions in his plays, we are apt to discover that every suggestion of surrealism is countered by a strong (or stronger) suggestion of a different or antithetical mode. If classical art is presumably created by a society or a social spokesman, then Shaw was often a classicist, for he mirrored Victorian and Edwardian society. If the romantic method extolled the autonomy of the artist, then Shaw was also a romantic who remained true to his own idiosyncratic creeds. So, too, if surrealism expressed a hostility to bourgeois self-satisfaction in life and literature, then Shaw was also a surrealist who expressed his thoughts and convictions with a high degree of candour.

Surrealism, undoubtedly, had its negative aspects - doom, occultism, suicide - but, for the most part, the surrealists were poets who, as Fowlie holds, sought to "accept the enigmas of existence and in daily living learn to transcend impotencies, defeats, contradictions, wars." (Fowlie 20) It is often bruited about that Shaw was really no systematic philosopher, that virtually every idea he promulgated was, in fact, derived from some other thinker, and that he was merely a sounding-board for diverse ideas. In this sense, he was more poet than philosopher and more surrealist than literalist, for Shaw is relevant today not because of his philosophy but because of his dramatic and comic parables. We do not read *Saint Joan* to learn about Catholic theology or philosophy. We do not read *Misalliance* to learn about Victorian or Edwardian educational philosophy. We do not go to *Heartbreak House* to learn about pessimism or nihilism. We do not turn to *Major Barbara* to become wiser about Salvationist belief. And we do not really experience *Man and Superman* as an ideologue's textbook on Creative Evolution. Each of these plays is a distinctive parable, which implies that it is an extended metaphor and, therefore, is something above mere realism. In each of them, Shaw's vision of existence is deeper, more intuitive, rawer than the vision of philosophers, and these plays survive because they have transcended their historical contexts.

Shaw demonstrated in these plays and in several others a surrealist inclination to free man from the constrictions of an excessively utilitarian, pragmatic, doctrinaire world. In each of the plays Shaw aimed at illumination after disillusionment, and this thrust towards surpassing ordinary experience and knowledge highlighted an enduring inner force. Shaw did not aim at speculative philosophy, nor did he aim at beautiful or ornamental art. In his Epistle Dedicatory to Arthur Bingham Walkley in *Man and Superman*, he wrote:

> My contempt for *belles lettres*, and for amateurs who become the heroes of the fanciers of literary virtuosity, is not founded on any illusion of mine as to the permanence of those forms of thought (call them opinions) by which I strive to communicate my bent to my fellows. ...No doubt I must

> recognize, as even the Ancient Mariner did, that I must tell
> my story entertainingly, if I am to hold the wedding guest
> spellbound in spite of the siren sounds of the loud bassoon.
> But 'for art's sake' alone I would not face the toil of writing
> a single sentence. I know that there are men who, having
> nothing to say and nothing to write, are nevertheless so in
> love with oratory and with literature that they delight in
> repeating as much as they can understand of what others
> have said or written aforetime. I know that the leisurely
> tricks which their want of conviction leaves them free to play
> with the diluted and misapprehended message supply them
> with a pleasant parlor game which they call style. I can pity
> their dotage and even sympathize with their fancy. But a true
> original style is never achieved for its own
> sake....Effectiveness of assertion is the Alpha and Omega of
> style. He who has nothing to assert has no style and can have
> none: he who has something to assert will go as far in the
> power of style as its momentousness and his conviction will
> carry him. Disprove his assertion after it is made, yet its
> style remains. (Shaw E xxxvi - xxxvii)

As we know from his express aversion to art for art's sake, Shaw
did not want plays to stop with aesthetics. And in this regard, he was like
the surrealists who wanted more reality than normally found in a logical
or beautifully ordered universe. And yet to ally Shaw with surrealism in
almost any way is to tempt critical outrage, for in no biography of Shaw
is there any explicit reference to such an alliance; indeed, there is scarcely
a reference to anything of the surrealist movement. However, I am not
asserting that Shaw was primarily a surrealist. I am simply claiming
(along with Christopher Newton) that several of his major works show
affinities with surrealism.

Now it is prudent to add that we can get to Shaw's surrealism
through Blake, Nietzsche, Marx, and Wagner rather than through Jarry,
Apollinaire, and Breton. Dick Dudgeon in *The Devil's Disciple* is, as
Shaw claimed in the play's preface, "an avowed Diabolonian." (Weintraub
141) Shaw explained Dudgeon's connection to John Bunyan, William
Blake, and Nietzsche:

> Two and a half centuries ago our greatest English dramatizer
> of life, John Bunyan, ended one of his stories with the
> remark that there is a way to hell even from the gates of
> heaven, and so led us to the equally true proposition that
> there is a way to heaven even from the gates of hell. A
> century ago William Blake was, like Dick Dudgeon, an

avowed Diabolonian: he called his angels devils and his devils angels. His devil is a Redeemer. Let those who have praised my originality in conceiving Dick Dudgeon's strange religion read Blake's Marriage of Heaven and Hell, and I shall be fortunate if they do not rail at me for a plagiarist. But they need not go back to Blake and Bunyan. Have they not heard the recent fuss about Nietzsche and his Good and Evil Turned Inside Out? (Weintraub 141)

And it is Nietzsche's form that hovers palpably in the backgrounds of *Major Barbara, Man and Superman*, and *Heartbreak House*, and more dimly behind the figures of *Saint Joan* and Julius Caesar (both of whom are superhuman in a Nietzschean sense because they create their own ethics), just as Karl Marx has some bearing on Shaw's socialism.

Blake and Nietzsche introduced the possibility of the marvellous in art and literature - Blake by his visionary symbolism, and Nietzsche by his concept of the formidable *Übermensch*. And by making not only some of his men but also some of his women superhuman, Shaw was indulging a surrealist vision of the marvellous transformation of human destiny. The superman or superwoman in Shaw exercises an extraordinary ability for revolutionary love, wisdom, and action. Shaw's New Woman (particularly Saint Joan, Ann Whitefield, Lina Szczepanowska, Ellie Dunn) are like the surrealist heroine of Man Ray or Paul Delraux - the mysterious female who "holds the key to man's destiny," and one who is to be approached "in a mood of anguished expectancy." Through her love or protection, "man may hope for paradise regained. Through woman he may dream of regeneration." (Matthews 159) As Matthews asserts in this regard: "Woman is capable of giving life meaning, of elevating it to significance, because she possesses the power to mediate between man and the marvellous." (Matthews 163)

But what was the marvellous in Shaw? Apart from the obvious instances of the recondite, supernatural, or visionary - the spirit of Hecate behind *Heartbreak House*, the Epilogue of *Saint Joan*, the blurring of dream and reality in *Caesar and Cleopatra*, the Day of Judgement in *The Simpleton of the Unexpected Isles*, the dream in Hell in *Man and Superman*, the Dionysian satire in *Major Barbara* - the obvious marvel was Shaw's use of paradox, for here Shaw manifested an anarchic tension between his puritanical background and his urge for metaphysical rebellion. Shaw was able to see both sides of a coin at once, and to argue a proposition and its contrary with equal force and conviction. Paradox was his great weapon, and paradox appears anarchic even as it archly carves out meaning. "The golden rule is that there are no golden rules." (Shaw E

227)   So, Shaw was able to be hostile to conscience while being conscientiously moral, and to be a critic of Don Juan while practising his own brand of Don Juanism in his sex life. As G.K. Chesterton argued, Shaw's was "a worried and conscientious anarchy." (Irvine 141)

Shaw could not, of course, be a true anarchist. He was too much conditioned by Victorian puritanism to break completely free from the conventions of his world. However, there was marvellous tension in some of his plays as a result of the puritan's dreaming himself into adventures of mind and soul. In his most mature period, Shaw made speculative plunges into the future, producing at times a remarkable "otherworldliness."   William Irvine traces Shaw's course upon an "inward world of meditation" and surmises that "as Don Juan, Shaw looked forward with confidence to what ideas - and eugenics - might ultimately achieve,"; that as Peter Keegan, he began to see his world of ideas threatening to turn into a world of dreams; and that "as Barbara, he experienced a final sharp disillusionment with the life of the spirit." (Irvine 244) In *Heartbreak House, Back to Methuselah*, and *The Simpleton of the Unexpected Isles* Shaw became almost overwhelmingly metaphysical and cosmic, but even as he did, he allowed bright flashes of the marvellous to impress his meaning on audiences.

Newton first sensed Shaw's surrealism when he began to direct *Misalliance* for his inaugural season in 1980. However, it was not until his 1983 production of *Caesar and Cleopatra* that he and his designer Cameron Porteous actually realized that they were on to something radically significant in Shavian interpretation. It was during *Caesar and Cleopatra* that the two discussed surrealist images, using the American artist Joseph Cornell as an inspiration for the design. Cornell had made his mark by creating Shadow Boxes - perhaps two inches or three inches deep, a foot high, and two feet wide - inside of which were stunningly evocative abstract or surrealist statements about moments in time and space. Actually, Cornell's association with surrealism had begun in the thirties when he began arranging found objects in glass and wooden boxes, creating three dimensional collage constructions that were forerunners of the highly popular Assemblage genre in the fifties and sixties.

Influenced by Max Ernst, Miro, and (especially) Duchamp - though without Duchamp's comic sense - Cornell aimed at a "poetic picture," dissolving structure with surrealist atmosphere that had an intense metaphorical potential. He used such diverse objects as maps, balls, butterflies, figurines, springs, cards, papers, jars, glass, photo-engravings, feathers, compasses, marbles, toys, pipes, dried flowers, and mirrors - all to create "a historical present which sees through the cultural past."

(*Contemporary Artists* 206) Deeply interested in history, Cornell wanted to demonstrate the interrelatedness of objects past and present. However, his mode of surrealism depended on a smallness of scale and on seduction rather than on shock tactics.

As Brian O'Doherty remarks of the Shadow Boxes, the atmosphere "acknowledges the surface as flat, yet makes an infinite depth accessible." (O'Doherty 274) The particular combination of literalism and illusion makes for a surrealist homage to nostalgia, as well as a meditation on mortality. The found objects evoke an historical past, and their presence is an image of memory itself, but they are, of themselves, only relics that bear information of that past. However, when placed in Cornell's idiosyncratic configurations - even though these are in miniature - they are avatars of themes, such as isolation, innocence, enigma, transience, voyages, et cetera, all connected by imagery, mood, light, and colour to symbolism.

Newton and Porteous had already explored Cornell's concept of surrealism at the Vancouver Playhouse, and now Newton wanted a design for *Caesar and Cleopatra* which would suggest an intriguing dichotomy: the reality of the play would take place *inside* a box, while the reality of the theatre would take place *outside* the box. So, Porteous devised a series of working sketches showing how the play would come together around strong images. Porteous stole a metaphor from the fifth earl of Caernavon, the famed Egyptologist, whose most famous discovery in excavating in the Valley of the Kings from 1906-1923 was the tomb of Tutankhamen. When Caernavon opened up the tomb, he is reported to have said in awe: "I have seen the most glorious things." Porteous wanted his audiences to feel that they, too, were looking into a tomb and seeing the most glorious things. The geometry and iconography of the boxed sets had, in fact, a connection with one of Cornell's boxes about Cleopatra. Cornell's composition had paralleled Egyptian involvement with the tomb and after-life, for it contained oddments that showed the ancient custom of securing articles most required by the deceased in the after-life. (O'Doherty 276) Porteous' iconography was bounded by tomblike walls, and the suggestion was sometimes unmistakably of a mausoleum reliquary - grand, formal, but distanced by time and isolation.

Porteous created a pedestalled Sphinx that would not fit into the box, but which, as Shaw indicated in his directions in Act One, would spread "in infinite fearless vigil" on the sands against an almost fantastically radiant blue sky. "There's nothing naturalistic about a sphinx too big to get into a box. It created one of the most powerful opening moments I've ever experienced in a theatre for a long time." What Porteous and Newton created, in effect, was a heightened reality of feeling or mood through light and shape, and the extraordinarily poetic image of Marti Maraden's childlike Cleopatra asleep on a heap of red poppies between the great paws of the Sphinx led into a surreal dreamlike moment - like something out of a Rousseau painting.

Newton had seen Poynter's painting of Joseph and Mary during their retreat from Egypt, in which the holy couple spend a night on the desert sands in the paws of a sphinx. He based his whole production concept on that single image. Porteous remarked to Newton: "It's very much the way we do our work. We both have a very good grasp on the history of art. And paintings inspire our intellect to think about life." At the time, Newton was also very keen on Alma Tadema, whose genre and sexuality fitted into his concept of Shavian sexuality.

"Why do we say Shaw is the great surrealist?" Porteous wonders aloud, answering his own question with a reference to Shaw's notes at the end of the first scene in Act One. Caesar, who does not divulge his real identity to the girlishly innocent Cleopatra, asks her to lead him to her throne-room. Terrified of the Romans and of her image of Caesar as a cannibal, she is only too glad to get away from the desert to her palace. Shaw writes:

> He follows her, the bucina sounding louder as they steal across the desert. The moonlight wanes: the horizon again shows black against the sky, broken only by the fantastic silhouette of the Sphinx. The sky itself vanishes in darkness, from which there is no relief until the gleam of a distant torch falls on great Egyptian pillars supporting the roof or a majestic corridor....They come down the corridor, Caesar peering keenly about at the strange architecture ....Further along....a spacious transept in which Caesar sees....a throne, and behind the throne a door. (Shaw B 206)

This is a most cinematic scene-change, which requires a type of dissolve and a slow fade-in to a new setting. Nevertheless, Porteous (aided by Jeffrey Dallas' virtuoso lighting) was able to realize the change in such terms that made it a virtual phantasmagoria. By the use of technology, the Sphinx just vanished upstage with a puff of smoke, and a wall closed in, while Douglas Rain's Caesar and Marti Maraden's Cleopatra merely stood, turned slowly, and were then suddenly in a new setting. Porteous draws a connection between the surrealist visuals and Shaw's text: "Maybe it's not surrealist in the true sense of the word, but certainly there's a heightened reality to the way he uses his language and how he pitches his ideas about."

The stage floor was actually taken from a Tadema painting. It was a creamy marble effect with terra cotta inlays, and the shape of the inlays was important because Ftateeta's suicide behind the giant statue of Ra was turned into a horrific surreal event by having blood suddenly pour out at the bottom of Ra's pedestal and flow right around the perimeter of the set on the red of the inlay. In effect, what Cleopatra was seeing was the statue bleeding. And that was what sent her into shrieking horror.

This larger-than-life, virtually hallucinatory or phantasmagoric reality was extended to the final act (the shortest of the five in the play) when the harbour is dominated by Caesar's galley. Newton did not want a mere Victorian finale, a walkdown as in a pantomime. Caesar's goodbye to Cleopatra and to Egypt acquired a different resonance by the image of the galley filling the rear space of the boxed set. All that the audience saw was part of the side of the ship. It was as if the galley was so large that in close-up all we saw was wood blotting out sky and perversely refusing to be contained by the geometry of the box. Only a few gigantic oars could fit the box. Keenly sensitive to the irony of Caesar's farewell (Caesar promises to send Cleopatra "a man, Roman from head to heel and Roman of the noblest ...brisk and fresh, strong and young, hoping in the morning, fighting in the day, and revelling in the evening" -- Shaw B 304), Newton was quick to capitalize on the idea of a scene with a box-within-a-box, so that the audience would be forced to reflect on the meaning and point of view of the moment. "You have to ask yourself: 'Through whose eyes are you seeing this moment? Where is our attention? How is Shaw engineering where our attention is? Is it in the place where we think we should be looking? Should we be looking at it through another eye at the moment?'"

The finale had a sweet sadness to it, for Caesar was bidding farewell to an entire civilization, and Cleopatra was saturated with mixed emotions - relief at a conqueror's departure, yet sadness at the loss of a great tutor. To convey this mood, Newton used background music of Dvorak's Prague Waltzes. This deliberate anachronism was not meant to be weird, but to sound lush with the rich sophistication of another culture, so that when the audience heard the huge sweep of strings into the waltzes, it also felt a special kind of pulse - one bred of two incredibly rich cultures. And the conjunction of Dvorak, ancient Egypt, ancient Rome, and Shavian Victorianism supported a vision of the past as something that could be connected to the present. The music became an additional metaphor to the visual surrealism of décor, and a reminder of a dramatic journey for Caesar and Cleopatra - a journey marked by a rich variety of things in poetic relationship to heightened consciousness. The generated sentiment was not opposed to surrealism, for surrealism has always found most of its material in bourgeois objects and images, such as the trivia and relics of Victorian parlours.

Dan Laurence was first completely baffled by Newton's approach, but when he saw the production, he knew exactly what Newton was doing. Laurence realized that Newton was feeling his way to being able to present Shaw's plays for modern audiences without destroying the integrity of the pieces. And, even more than this, Newton was illuminating aspects of Shaw - his real feeling, heightened sense of reality (sometimes delicately poetic), strange blendings of fantasy and reality, sexuality - that academic and theatre critics were not quick to understand.

CHAPTER THREE

MISALLIANCE (1980)

In choosing to direct *Misalliance* as his first Shavian exercise, Newton may well have wished to serve notice to Shavian purists that the Festival would no longer be old-fashioned or glitteringly didactic in its approach to Shaw. At first glance, *Misalliance* may not seem the ideal choice by which to set a new course at Niagara-on-the-Lake where Shaw's reputation appeared to have been based chiefly on a combination of brilliant talk, disquisition, and japery, but certainly not on theatrical allegory. The play is really an elaborate one-acter, with no change of scene, and it is dense with talk and argument on a number of topics-- children, parents, education, romance, commerce, politics, civilization, religion--which sometimes appear to stifle the dramatic and comic action.

Most critics treat this play as Shaw's provocative elaboration on the theme of education and children, perhaps because they pin their interpretation chiefly on Shaw's own preface which he called "A Treatise On Parents And Children." As was his wont, Shaw began his preface with airy generalizations and scattered examples, pressing his treatise but possibly misleading his readers about the scope of his play. Those who take him at his word in the treatise quickly miss his real points about education and children, which are not simply that Victorian English schools are dull, morbid, and cruel, or that children, who are infinitely perfectible, are coerced into docility and unimaginativeness. His real points are about the general character of the English people as a whole. Viewing childhood as "a stage in the process of that continual remanufacture of the Life Stuff," Shaw considers a child to be an experiment-- "a fresh attempt to produce the just man made perfect: that is, to make humanity divine." However, he argues, English society makes moral monsters of children, beginning in the home where parents interfere with their offspring's characters and attempt to force them into their own very restrictive moulds. The typical English school - or, rather, that which Shaw holds to be typical - continues this insidious process to enslavement by functioning more as a prison than as a place of imaginative liberation. Here coercion becomes "a despicable routine," with the school conspiring, as it were, with the home and society to "keep people in ignorance and error, so that they may be incapable of successful revolt" against their domestic, academic, and industrial slavery. English civilization, as a whole - but particularly in its colonial manifestations - has functioned and thrived on the way of intimidation. The result for English society has been a nation divided roughly into bullies and their drudges, with intellectual and moral laziness and ignorance being the shared attributes of each group. The typical Englishman, then, shuns the invention of new ideas or the expanding domain of knowledge, and insists on ready-made routines.

Shaw's conclusion is one more of common sense than of radical novelty, for it is based on an aversion to compulsion of any sort. Shaw argues for a reconciliation of education with liberty, identifying the "crux of the whole difficulty about parents, schoolmasters, priests, absolute monarchs, and despots of every sort" with "the tendency to abuse national docility."

The play itself is a working-out in a very general way of these seminal ideas, though it is not an unpleasant satire on marriage, the family, education, and capitalism - interrelated themes which add up to a criticism of contemporary English civilization. The play is more memorable for its characters than for its plot, for it has the middle-class Tarleton family where the husband is a very successful entrepreneur in the underwear business, who prides himself on his eclectic reading (everything from the Bible, Pepys, and Shakespeare to Dickens, Darwin, and Chesterton), and where the wife is an authoritarian but simple woman, brimming with bromides and platitudes. The daughter Hypatia is a bit of a ferocious predator when her right male prey appears, and the son Johnny is a vacuous mercenary, a chump with no pretensions to culture. Their houseguests are Lord Summerhays, once a colonial governor, who is still steeped in the imperial values of Empire, and his son Bentley, a brilliant intellectual with the incongruous body of a weakling. Bentley is engaged to Hypatia, who scorns him and rejects the secret proposal of his father. The situation is altered by a plane crash, which literally drops two visitors into the scene: a beautiful Polish circus acrobat called Lina Szczepanowska (who also immediately calls for a Bible and six oranges) and her companion, Joey Percival, who turns out to have been a college friend of Bentley and who has three "fathers." The accident propels the farce into fantastical areas of action - especially with the intrusion of a socialist-anarchist clerk out for revenge against Tarleton - and the play sometimes reels with the Tarleton and Summerhays males all pursuing Lina in one form or another, and with Hypatia apparently following the dictates of her biological Life Force in chasing Percival through the woods.

Misalliance was not held in high repute by critics upon its initial appearance. *The Times* described it as "the debating society of a lunatic asylum - without a motion, and without a chairman." (Holroyd B 244) Desmond MacCarthy felt that Shaw "had not a clear notion where his perceptions in this case were leading him." (Holroyd B 244) Max Beerbohm objected to "the unreality, the remoteness from human truth, that pervades the whole 'debate.'...a debate, to stand the test of the theatre, must have some central point, and it must be progressive, must be about something, and lead to something. *Misalliance* is about anything and everything." (Holroyd B 244) The general critical consensus was that it was one of Shaw's tedious discussion plays - a misconception that even so notable a critic as Maurice Valency has furthered by his ill-considered dismissal of the comedy as "a tolerably dull entertainment based on an aimless narrative." (Valency 292)

Misalliance has, fortunately, risen in critical stock in our time, although it is still not often done full justice by critics and directors who fail to see its connections with witty symbolists such as Pirandello, Ionesco, and Orton, or its Edwardian allegory on the subject of the modern world. One of the best Shavian critics, Margery M. Morgan, articulates Shaw's affinity with Pirandello: "As surely as Pirandello, Shaw deserves credit for shattering the old theatre of illusion and the tight structure of the well-made play to let in more life. In the series of plays that continues from *Misalliance*, through *Heartbreak House*, to *Too True To Be Good* and *The Simpleton Of The Unexpected Isles*, he jests among the ruins he has made. But he is a cunning jester, only apparently irresponsible; like Pirandello again, he offers a personal and meaningful dramatic form where convention-dimmed eyes see only chaos." (Morgan 187)

Newton's 1980 production, designed by Cameron Porteous, stayed closer to a reading of the play as a satire on education, the family, and capitalism, than to one of the play as a vaster allegory. But his production also stressed the romance. The set itself was a very light sienna plaster colour with green Art Nouveau stencilling. The floor was red terra cotta - almost like big reg Spanish tiles. The set showed a conservatory with awnings to keep the shade down, large glass patio windows and door, and established an upscale, fairly modern version of turn-of-the-century Viennese architecture. The set gave more height and tone to what is usually seen as a stuffy little conservatory. The geometry was based on double diagonals, and the set was deliberately off-centre so that it came rushing at the audience. Porteous created tall willows in the garden, backlit by Jeffrey Dallas in a method similar to what is called contra lighting in Europe. Josef Svoboda is a key proponent of such lighting, and his light-walls or light-curtains have distinguished many European productions. Dallas' lighting produced a strong feeling of daylight pouring in through windows, and imparted a feeling that was quite different from the standard one of productions that use conventional white glass of the Victorian era.

Porteous' costume palette evoked a sense of Viennese colour. The young men were in white cricket flannels. Percival was in light brown and canvas hues. Tarleton wore very soft, checked knickerbockers. Mrs. Tarleton was in a velvet Biedemeier green with an Art Nouveau cut. This gave her maturity, strength, and an association with gardening. Pink showed up in some of the conservatory flowers and in some of the other properties, but the strongest pink was in Hypatia's dress, establishing her innocence and bringing to mind young, blooming sexuality - the first blush of a pink rose. Hypatia's pink and Mrs. Tarleton's green were the strongest colours, and their opposition set up intriguing ideas of youthful sexuality in conflict with social decorum.

Tarleton was played by Sandy Webster as a fuzzy-voiced, knickerbockered shop-owner with pretensions to eclectic learning. Although he believed he was a man of ideas - all second-hand ones at that - this Tarleton was more credibly a capitalist: "There's money in me, madam, no matter what I go into." As his wife, Marion Gilsenan allowed her distaste for the upper-classes to be superceded only by her money-consciousness, although her warm maternalism was certainly suggested in the scenes with the bungling anarchist Gunner.

The play could be divided into three large movements: the first being an overture of themes and discussions, the second a faster section of unexpected complications; and the third being a mixed coda of brisk, yet sometimes meditative, notes. In the first movement, Newton carefully emphasized the motifs of money and the often intractable relationships of parents and children. The opening scene between Bentley Summerhays and Johnny Tarleton was an exposition that counterpointed a Tarleton who was the true scion of his father, and a Summerhays who was a paradoxical mutation of his parent. Peter Hutt's Johnny, in costume very close to that of his father, shared his father's pride in business. James

Rankin's Bentley, capering at the crated Turkish bath, imitating jungle sounds, provoking Johnny to violent anger, and screaming for help when threatened with retaliation, was all brains and weak body. Fundamentally an idler who was thoroughly disliked by his peers because of his cheeky impudence and conceit, he was the "spoilt young pup" to Johnny's brutish bully.

While each of these young men was a foil to the other, Deborah Kipp's Hypatia was an utter foil to them both. She was clearly misallied with Bentley, her suitor, and was quite clearly fed up with respectability and money, though the actress did not suggest her banked "fires," nor was she compelling enough in voice or appearance to convince us that Hypatia could turn into a really interesting "active verb."

The appearance of Lord Summerhays on the scene set another note in place on questions of generation and value. A former colonial governor, he is well versed in the rhetoric and tactics of imperial coercion, plumping for fraud and force when subtle suasion does not work to his advantage. In this regard, he typifies the radical humbug and rottenness of English civilization and, so, belongs in the stuffy Tarleton house where dogmatism sometimes tries to enforce docility, and where old clichés die hard. David Dodimead made an effective Summerhays, an old talker now decayed with shrinking from modern reality.

The second movement begins with the airplane crash in the garden, which results in the advent of the extraordinary Lina Szczepanowska and the very unusual Joey Percival. These two strangers are catalysts for the action or, more importantly, for the changes in attitude. Lina captivates all the men, young and old, of the household, while Joey activates the biological Life Force in Hypatia, who promptly chases him up hills and into the heather, until he reverses things to become her pursuer. When a third unexpected visitor materializes in the convulsively bungling form of the world-be assassin Gunner, this middle movement spins off into wonderful social and philosophical comedy, pitting anarchist against imperialists, slave against his masters. Unfortunately, Andrew Gillies' portrayal of Gunner lacked comic inspiration - except for a brief and extraneous bit of business with his bowler hat - and the role appeared to fall a little flat.

Geraint Wyn-Davies, however, was a handsome Joey Percival, modulating from romantic charm or panic to crisp intimidation or benign resolve. He looked, indeed, like the most satisfactory specimen of youth. And Carole Shelley, although not physically strong enough to be an aerialist, certainly exuded a charisma as Lina, and phrased her comedy sharply so that we could be convinced of her enchanting power to make real men of the males.

The third movement records the decisive changes in the Tarleton and Summerhays families. Newton's sustained use of his actors in relaxed seated or strolling positions indicated a generally idle, leisurely class, which made Bentley's caperings and tantrums, Hypatia's bursts of romantic tag with Joey, and Lina's vocal and physical "attack" all the more interesting as part of the choreography and dialectic. Upon discovering Joey's financial inability to support her, Hypatia asks her father to "buy the brute" for her. Tarleton, portraying himself as a wronged Lear, launches into a litany of complaints against the young. Lord Summerhays, who had tried to woo Hypatia by promising her an early widowhood, and who had appealed to Lina to protect their Viennese alliance of two years ago, is an elegant, vanishing aristocrat, quite unable to deal with human beings except by coercion or bribery.

The atmosphere certainly seemed unhealthy, and Lina's disgust at the pervasive love-sickness in this "rabbit hutch" was palpably justified. Shelley came to the fore in her climactic aria on the house and its characters, with the others becoming a rapt audience for her set-piece - an injunction to Bentley to dare! - which is really Shaw's puritanical version of the Life Force curled at the edges to seem revolutionary.

Jeffrey Dallas' lighting plot included a descending darkness in the final movement, beginning fairly early and deepening into something between dusk and the fell of night. If this was supposed to indicate the darkness of inherent intellectual and spiritual dullness, it succeeded admirably. The production became a comedy on purchase: characters could be bought directly (Percival) or indirectly (Gunner), alliances could be seen as offers to purchase (Lord Summerhays and Hypatia; Tarleton and Lina) or as those transcending purchase (Lina and Bentley).

And what of the subject of education which so permeated Shaw's own preface? Newton's production revealed the education of all the characters, to varying degrees and ends, though it also showed a fundamentally unchanged Johnny and Mrs. Tarleton and a Lord Summerhays who would never understand his own son. Hypatia and Bentley had had a breakthrough in their lives, and Tarleton himself, while not daring enough to disengage himself from his shop or public libraries and ascend to the empyrean with Lina and Bentley, was no longer as self-assured as he once was. By the end, he was a wavering, uncertain figure, out of talk, though probably rocked to the core by the remarkable manifestation of the Life Force. The delicious irony in the play is that the changes or plain shocks are delivered by a woman who, in truth, is very much a schoolteacher in her brisk, authoritative, prescriptive manner!

This 1980 production did not receive many enthusiastic reviews, perhaps because it did not strike enough sparks in the casting or interpretation. The romance elements were somewhat reduced by Deborah Kipp's brass tacks voice - though this quality worked well for her battles with Marion Gilsenan's Mrs. Tarleton, and for her impassioned frustration at her family's preoccupation with "respectability" - and by Carole Shelley's raw, broad Polish accent, although here, too, it should be added that Shelley's forceful acting made an emphatic case for a life of dangerous risks. Shelley made an effective foil, too, for James Rankin's overdone Bentley and David Dodimead's coolly varnished Summerhays.

The comic elements were also somewhat mixed in effect, with Andrew Gillies' Gunner not up to his big moments with the confused recantation or even up to the general impression of a nervous gunman prompted either to hysterical tears or to rhetoric of neurotic bravado. James Rankin's Bentley missed the real curve of a credible human being, turning the character's fit of sobbing at the loss of Hypatia into a livid spectacle of wild, frantic hopping about, foot-stamping, and screaming and kicking from the floor.

Newton's biggest contribution to a re-interpretation of *Misalliance* lay in focus on the dialectic of bound and free spirits, and in the flow of fairy-tale and legend that he created. This *Misalliance* turned out to be about the education of *men* who learn that there are thrilling, adventurous ways of transcending the barrenness and decay of their old, familiar ways of life. The production's blocking culminated in a final moment with only three characters on stage - Lina, Bentley, and Tarleton - and this image probably aimed at sealing the impression of an almost mythic force, for Lina is the wonder woman who inspires males of two different generations to desires and declarations quite beyond their normal limits. Lina, who has agitated every male in the house by her charismatic Life Force, prepares to ascend once again like a goddess, taking Bentley with her, and tempting Tarleton into wishing he could accompany them.

Despite its inventiveness, this *Misalliance* showed a Newton who was still fairly cautious, though not reverential, in his treatment of Shaw. He did not attempt to magnify the comedy's bold surrealistic elements - those that show submerged Euripedean elements. As Margery Morgan shows, the shadow of *The Bacchae* hovers above Shaw's comedy, for the pavilion setting of Tarleton's house, with its urns, alcohol, and arched semi-circle of pillars, implies a temple of false art as well as a temple of Bacchus. Lina's nature (with its miracle and mystery in the image of her as a tightrope artist and aviatrix fallen out of the sky) has a divine touch about it. Hypatia pursues Percival through the woods as if in maenadic abandon, and Gunner's assault on the Tartletons is accomplished under the influence of sloe gin (a Bacchic cup). Moreover, the Turkish bath in which he hides and from where he spies on Hypatia's frenzy (in a correspondence with Pentheus' spying on Bacchic orgies) is a focal point. Tarleton himself can be regarded as a Cadmus figure, boasting as he does of his youthful spirit in a middle-aged body, and in his joining with the others in ritual celebrations. The climactic airplane crash which shatters the glass of the pavilion and destroys the greenhouse, is "Shaw's version of the shaking of the Theban palace and the destruction of its outbuildings. The binding of the god, on the orders of Pentheus, is represented in the capture and intimidation of the Gunner." (Morgan 195) Finally, Lina's departure in a machine with Bentley is more Greek than English, as are the choric interludes and unity of scene. (Morgan 195)

These associations with Euripedes show some of the screens through which the comedy can be viewed, and they are more than enough to reward the enterprising director who would aim for a symbolic production. But Newton avoided them. His overall approach, while certainly not without its own charms and audacity, fell somewhere in the middle between drawing-room farce and the heightened leaps of imagination in Shaw's depiction of anarchic feelings, thoughts, and actions. *Misalliance* is a comedy with a rich variety of forces that appear to thrive on their paradoxical idiosyncrasies. However, in Newton's hands, Shaw's surrealistic distortion of romantic and comic conventions was softened, at best. Its potent character would not emerge until Newton's second *Misalliance* a decade later.

CHAPTER FOUR

SAINT JOAN

Newton provoked controversy and outrage with his production of *Saint Joan* in 1981. He announced that he would cut the Epilogue. "We tried it in the early rehearsals," he explained to Herman Trotter of *The Buffalo News*, "but found there was no way it would fit with the way we're doing the rest of the play. It's really Shaw at his worst, joking, pulling back from points already made and hitting you over the head with ideas already presented." The text was not sacred to him. Newton did have some critics on his side. William Irvine, James Agate, and even Shaw's biographer Archibald Henderson considered the Epilogue to be redundant, and others, such as Brooks Atkinson, have thought it to "snatch a fine play back into theatre tedium." (Beckerman and Siegman 174) Shavian purists, however, raised a hue and cry that resounded across North America and the Atlantic. "Without the Epilogue, it is a damaged work of art," protested Dan Laurence. "What the audience gets is not Shaw's play. It's Newton's play." Laurence prompted the Society of Authors in England, which holds the rights to Shaw's plays, to take action, and this body refused permission to the Festival to present the play without the Epilogue. Newton retreated from his audacious position, but not without firing back at his critics for their "attack on our integrity," and condemning "a threat from academia who want to keep Shaw on a library shelf. It's an attempt to freeze a man who was interested in life."

Newton's second controversy was his choice of then little-known Nora McLellan for the title-role. McLellan had arrived at the Shaw Festival in 1980 to do Brecht's *A Respectable Wedding*, and one night

Newton asked: "Would you like to play Saint Joan next season?" She laughed: "Of course! That's cute. Let's get you another drink." The next day she called him up and asked: "Were you serious?" When assured that he was, she still doubted him. Few in Canada could believe it. "There was a great 'Are you kidding?' because I was known as a singer. I was working hard on being an actress, but I was noted for musicals. There was a famous director in Canada who tried to talk me out of doing Joan. He said, 'I think it's the worst thing that's ever happened to you.'" (Hill 212)

Newton did not seem deterred by the fact that the role, in terms of what an actress is required to possess in the way of stamina, intelligence, passion, and technique, is Shaw's equivalent of Shakespeare's Hamlet. He wanted someone who was not afraid of just lumbering out on the stage and being aggressive and masculine. But although McLellan had developed a comic technique and had stage presence, she was not yet, in the critics' minds, ready for Shaw's religious and military genius. Newton tried to defend his choice in the press by pointing to her comic sense which, he believed, would benefit a role that some knew could easily become "a piteous little waif in her misery, and too much of a darling in armour at other moments," as Desmond MacCarthy had said of Madame Ludmilla Pitoeff's performance in 1930, (MacCarthy 172-173) or "half angel and half bird...with a gentleness and ineffability unknown to celestial choir or cooing dove," as was said of Sarah Bernhardt's performance in Jules |Barnier's *Jeanne D'Arc* in 1889. (Agate 214) Newton said of McLellan: "Also important is the fact that she's large enough to wield a sword and be physically commanding. Wispy Joans don't wash." And he added for Jamie Portman: "To let someone like Nora do it and to set loose the passion is what this play needs. We want to treat Shaw on the level he should be dealt with - not as a wind-up orator but as a living, breathing human being writing about living, breathing people."

Saint Joan is not a chronicle play, nor is it a true tragedy. The play, as Eric Bentley has maintained, (and as Shaw hinted) is divided into "a Romance (scenes I, II, III), a Tragedy (Scenes IV, V, VI), and a Comedy (the Epilogue)." (Bentley A 172) There are numerous pantomime conventions, as Margery Morgan has indicated, that keep the heroine as "an enigma challenging the mind, never quite a tragic heroine or a victim whose boldness is finally pathetic." (Morgan 251) Morgan lists the conventions: the first scene with its "blustering baron and hens that won't lay, the nicknames, Polly and Jack and Dick the Archer," the comic abuse, and "the cool high-handedness of the girl with her feudal lord ('I have arranged it all: you have only to give the order') establish the relation to Christmas pantomime quite firmly, before the final absurd 'miracle' - 'The hens are laying like mad, sir. Five dozen eggs!' - sets its seal on the style.'' (Morgan 251) Then there are the figures of Bluebeard, Joan ''in the usual masculine garb of the Principal Boy,'' ''a refinement on the type of Jack or Dick (who grows up to play Widow Twankey),'' and the language she speaks. The clowning Dauphin, and the appearance and manners of Tremouille (''old Gruff-and-Grum'') and the Duchess (''an Ugly Sister, perhaps'') all point to a comic tradition, as does the role of de Stogumber. Moreover, the Epilogue, with Joan revealed as innocent fool in a way, reasserts the pantomime connection.

Newton's production did not scant the comedy, though the ensemble gave it a robustly coarse or febrile texture within an austere visual framework. There were no cardboard sets, no rich pageant of costumes, very few props. The first scene, in the castle of Vaucouleurs, had exceedingly dim lighting, and not the usual sunny stone castle chamber with a thirteenth-century mullioned window or a corner turret with a narrow arched doorway. The audience first heard a din which seemed to come from below the stage, before a shaft of light picked out Robert de Baudricourt crawling out and launching into the first bit of dialogue with his Steward on the cellar steps. The first spoken notes were a strident ''Shut up!'' to the roistering crew below. There was a dark, cold feeling, a mediaeval austerity, with a dog's barking to add to the din. Newton made free cuts in the text, which did no damage to the play, and his blocking was a way of showing that Joan is not really the principal incarnated idea in the play. Nora McLellan's first lines were delivered on the cellar steps leading to the Baudricourt's chamber. It was a weak introduction to the character, despite the actress' brassy voice, because, visually, she was given no predominance. The controlling notes of her performance were set in this scene: a quick, excited vocal delivery; a plain, unadorned religious spirit; a strident self-assurance on everything except her education. Asked her surname, she hesitated over the word, clearly indicating her illiteracy. Otherwise, she was a tough, determined, bossy young maiden, with her short, spikey hair, and her untidy, masculine dress. Not quite ''one of Mr. Arnold Bennett's 'managing young woman,'' as Agate put it (Agate 215), and certainly not a religious zealot yearning for martyrdom. She was simply an abnormal individual, a genius, perhaps, of military bravado, but a product of her times of cold, hard want, superstition, and fear. In terms of social and religious forces, she was not a principal player, merely a brisk upstart of extraordinary self-assurance, a peasant with a mission.

It was clear that Newton was not going to treat the play reverently as an Edwardian curio with social bric-à-brac. Of course, he knew the Shaw's histories are meant to rub off on our period, for they are full of spiritual anachronisms even when Shaw stays close to historical facts, but these incongruences are meant to connect with truths of our own time. As Desmond MacCarthy put it: "[Shaw] is confident that he has reached historic truth when he has succeeded in scratching historic characters till he finds beneath a modern man in fancy dress." (MacCarthy 163) Warwick, for instance, is not a mediaeval courtier, but a politically shrewd twentieth century aristocrat. De Stogumber is not a clerical secretary from the Middle Ages, but a ridiculous modern jingoist. And Joan herself is a very modern, young dissenter.

The sense of the modern was strongly compounded in Scene II, with a beginning worthy of Samuel Beckett in one of his sere, wordless sequences, as Jack Medley's Archbishop and Richard Farrell's La Tremouille came slowly out into a cold, windy room, in Chinon. There was a very long silence, broken only by the whining blasts of cold wind, the sound of rain coming through the roof, and the echo of footsteps running down corridors, all of which gave the moment a note of discomfort and edginess. Medley's slow, laborious putting up of his large umbrella, and Farrell's shivering in the cold dampness exacerbated the tension, fatigue, and boredom of the two visitors to Chinon, and added an existential absurdity, as if both men were waiting for some mediaeval Godot. This yielded to Shavian satire with the entrance of a vain Bluebeard, a rough La Hire, an extravagantly accoutered Duchess de la Tremouille, and an unstable Dauphin, part-man, part-child. Heath Lamberts' Dauphin and his cart - a pure invention by Newton and designer Cameron Porteous - supplied comic elements that offset Joan's detachment from the court. However, Lamberts' interpretation of the Dauphin as a nervously insecure, bumbling, cowardly, inarticulate figure was effected with such a broken vocal staccato and stutter that the scene did not flow as briskly as it could have, and Shaw's own deficient mediaeval atmosphere was displaced by the comic business: Joan's eager, high spirited unmasking of the Dauphin; the Dauphin's nervous retorts to intimidating courtiers; and the revelry of the stewards as they brought on the Dauphin's cart, a prop that became the very image of the king's "travelling show" referred to by Warwick in Scene IV.

But processions and processionals, which can sometimes dominate in productions of the play as much as any fustian, were not Newton's object. When he did indulge in them - as in Scene V at Rheims, which is organically musical and panoplied - the ceremonial movement described a world that was often detached from Joan or one that was extravagantly absurd. What Newton's production revealed was a focus on the tragedy of an individual who was out of sorts with her world because of a special mission that transcended conventions. Joan's morality clashes with the morality of Church, State, and even the Army, because she is a genius -

one whom William Irvine defined as "an instrument singled out by the Life Force to achieve progress, warring not against the evil of [one's] time but against its good, which from [one's] higher view appears evil." (Irvine 321) The trouble was that Nora McLellan did not make Joan extraordinary enough to be believable either as a genius or as a saint.

Shaw composed a rough, rural dialect for the part, which countless actresses have interpreted in a variety of English accents, ranging from North Country, Lumpshire, Irish, and West Country, to Yorkshire, Glaswegian, and Elizabethan. McLellan settled for Canadian - "a flat tone, very peasantish." (Hill 217) While this choice sealed the image of a very down-to-earth, untutored girl used to holding her own against either gender (in the first scene she quelled the loud, singing soldiers with a yell), it also stripped the text of musicality, giving an impression of a harsh instrument, and compelling the actress to find the romance by other physical means.

The third scene, on the south bank of the silver Loire, is part of the romantic phase of the play, resulting in a second miracle where Joan alters the course of the wind to Dunois' military advantage. This scene has a natural but spare pictorial beauty, with the elements of river, soft banks, Dunois' pennon and shield with its bend sinister, the flash of kingfisher, and a situation where the Maid begins to fascinate "the brave Dunois, the handsome Dunois, the wonderful invincible Dunois, the darling of all the ladies, the beautiful Bastard." Shaw attempts a rhetorical poetry that does not quite succeed. Desmond MacCarthy sums it up best: "Mr. Shaw cannot get poetry into his words. He has supreme gifts as a dramatist, insight and invention, generosity and fearlessness of mind; but when he calls upon the Muse of Words to do more for him than to define and state, she does not answer." (MacCarthy 173) Citing "excruciating false notes" in certain passages ("Drag about in a skirt," "the young lambs crying through the healthy frost," et cetera), MacCarthy complains: "This is the voice not of Jeanne d'Arc but of a suffragette and a cry from a garden city. 'Healthy frost!' Where has his imagination flown to? No mediaeval shepherdess would think the frost healthy."

Nora McLellan did not convert her audiences to a contrary view, nor did she attempt to do so, preferring, it seemed, to stress the Maid's mission and androgyny, and making it appear that the two were somehow intertwined.

The scene provided a good occasion to fuse the issues of sex and religious mission, for in Dunois' company, Joan is the most feminine figure on stage, if not an erotic interest. But she is also a virgin obsessed with a special purpose. As Margery Morgan contends, "there is a slight but definite touch of the troubadour about Dunois, as the blue flash of the kingfisher conspires to suggest that the coming of Joan to him, despite the disguise of her armour and bobbed hair and country bourgeois manner, has some quality of a visitation by the Virgin to her knight.'' (Morgan 255) The kingfisher is a traditional symbol of Christ (as used by Gerard Manley Hopkins and T.S. Eliot), and here it becomes "an attribute of the androgynous Shavian saint.''

The problem in Newton's production, however, was the quality and extent of the fusion. McLellan was certainly an androgynous figure - no wild beauty in cross-dress, but at least something like the Principal Boy of pantomime. She was aware of sex but had removed it from her desires, choosing to dress in male attire and to speak in a brusque, harsh manner. Newton helped her by his direction of the opening moments of the scene. Dunois was seen shaving and heard complaining about the wind in a sort of stumbling poetry: "West wind, west wind, west wind. Strumpet: steadfast when you should be wanton, wanton when you should be steadfast. West wind on the silver Loire: what rhymes to Loire?...West wind, wanton wind, wilful wind, womanish wind, false wind from over the water, will you never blow again?'' At this point his page appeared out of the water, covering his nakedness with a cloth and drying himself. When Joan appeared, the page was unaware of her gender until she responded to Dunois' naming of her as the Maid. The page's startled look and Joan's unblushing composure about his nakedness and Dunois' semi-nudity established Newton's point that Joan lived with and was indistinguishable from soldiers. McLellan fortified this by a lightly dismissive gesture after pointing to the page's crotch and saying matter-of-factly: "I do not care for the things women care for.'' Clearly, this young woman, who had prevailed against a breach of promise suit in Toulon, did not want to be thought of as a woman. She did not dress as one, nor did she dream of male lovers. Her one big dream was of leading a charge against the English at Orleans. She was, in fact and in McLellan's performance, a mediaeval daredevil.

Where McLellan failed in this scene, though it was only a slight failure in context, was as a functioning saint. Her Joan was identifiable with swords, guns, and battles; slightly less credible with sheep, meadows, and frost; and hardly convincing as a saint. Part of the reason was the actress' overemphasis of the girl's hectoring stubbornness and vehemence in a voice that often grated on the ear. Not that she needed a lovely RADA-trained voice for the monologues - which are really arias - but there is obviously more to Joan's vocal quality than a tomboyish assertiveness. It is true that Shaw does not assist an actress in this regard in the first three scenes, because he shows us Joan in a comic light more than in a religious one. But the subtext indicates a Joan who is instinctive, simplistic, and cheeky about her faith, and not someone who is as mischievous and bold as Peter Pan. As Margery Morgan says: "Joan is a figure of the exploring spirit, single and free," and "Shaw associates her with the air ('head in the sky'), with flight ('Are you afraid I will fly away?'), with freedom on the hills, in the light and the wind." (Morgan 256) Charles A. Berst adds: "Allegorically and historically, the sainthood of Joan is tied to her genius, with the credibility of her mystical role linked to the precocity and power of her natural talents." (Berst 267) Berst recognizes that "The issue of Joan's sainthood is developed through an impressive dramatic ambivalence in which scepticism complements conviction. Shaw builds the aesthetics of Joan's mystery by a subtle use of counterstatement. In Scene I he has Joan herself interpret her voices as coming from her imagination, and in every successive scene he qualifies mysticism by offering a commonsense explanation through one character or another. Rationalism beats in constant counterpoint to mysticism." (Berst 268)

One of the technical difficulties for an actress in the first three scenes is to suggest the impatience and intolerance of youth and the catalytic drive without overlaying the romantic aura of sainthood. Actually, there is nothing overtly saintly about Joan as yet, except her holy rebelliousness against the pomp, vanity, selfishness, and materialism of her social and religious superiors. Yet, beneath the surface comedy of boisterousness and bravado there is a special religious charge. Perhaps because we live in a sceptical age which characteristically downplays heroism, Newton and McLellan did not point up the religion except as a sort of high-energy obsession. Joan may very well have been a tomboy, but she must have known that she was radically different from other tomboys. She obviously had enormous spiritual potential as a teenager, and this aspect can be suggested on stage only by an openness that manages to bring out the best in other characters. However, with this openness goes a vocal technique that enables an actress to move up and down the scales without becoming monotonous or merely musical. It is analogous to playing the role of Juliet, where assured technique can support and enlarge the romantic undertones and overtones and sharpen the innate vulnerability of the characters.

Because the play is an ensemble-piece, Nora McLellan's deficiencies did not destroy the overall conception. The tragedy of Joan begins to be articulated with Scene IV in the English tent, where Warwick, Cauchon, and De Stogumber represent the institutional forces that will break Joan physically, mentally, and emotionally, and will almost crush her spirit, even though she is totally absent from the stage in this long, fascinating dialectical concerto of voices. When executed with technical polish and by actors with strong vocal instruments and intelligence, the scene is compelling, and what would otherwise seem like *longueurs* of long-winded orators become a brilliant orchestration of the forces arrayed against Joan. De Stogumber, the excited, jingoistic English chaplain, represents an exceedingly narrow orthodoxy with absolute categories of good and evil. He sees witchcraft in Joan (especially as her feats at Orleans where she walked alone with a white banner in hand after suffering what should have been a death-wound), and he abhors her for having usurped the divine authority of the Church and for having rebelled against England, her preferred example of true civilization. He is the most excitable of the trio, with the Earl of Warwick much pressed to stifle him, and with Bishop Cauchon urged to deflate him with ironic poise.

Warwick is the arch English politician-soldier, who propounds the feudal view of his time. He knows too well Joan's charismatic influence on the French army and her threat to the traditional social structure of the Middle Ages, and he would extinguish her only too readily once the Church has delivered her to the secular arm of the law. He is more patient than De Stogumber because he is used to devising political machinery for his own ends. Opposite him is Cauchon who is portrayed by Shaw not as an extremist ecclesiastic but as a fair-minded, rational Churchman with a sincere fear of spreading heresy. His true function is to save Joan from herself and from damnation as a heretic.

The tent scene began stormily, following the windy conclusion of Scene III on the Loire. To storm sounds, battle sounds, and trumpet moans, a huge canvas billowed and settled into the shape of a tent. When the lights came up - actually there was a backlit red to look like a fiery night in battle - the audience's eyes were drawn to emblems of the spoils of war - giant horses' heads in Grecian marble, large crucifixes, a piece of the Dauphin's cart, a huge chest with carvings, and a precious illuminated manuscript in the hands of De Stogumber. Barry MacGregor's chaplain was quick off the mark with his choleric, intemperate tirades and expostulations against Joan and the French. However, Robert Benson's Warwick played sleepily in a lazy legato that lowered both the energy and attack of the scene, especially when David Hemblen's Cauchon made extensive use of pauses and carefully measured cadences for his own long passages.

Newton attempted a little mood-making by a solitary offstage trumpet that sounded at various points in the concerto of voices, but which merely added a melancholy to what was already a heavy scene. The actors went for primary effects in characterization, with Barry MacGregor displaying the overly presumptuous imperiousness of the chaplain, Benson revealing the patient authority of the earl (though not enough of his foxiness), and Hemblen stressing the bishop's acute intellect and theological gravity. There was little overall shape to their rhetorical statements and counter-statements, and the effect was rather lackadaisical. However, Shaw's polemical points - even with Newton's editing - were not lost. The scene is virtually actor-proof, and it has a crucial part in the structure of the play, for in pinpointing Joan as a Protestant and Nationalist, it suggests that she is at the mercy of a new epoch bristling with legal, sacerdotal, and regal forces.

The next two scenes demonstrate Shaw's ability to build his climaxes, deepen the tragic notes, yet maintain an abstract musicality in his textual design. As William Irvine notes, Scene V is "constructed like a piece of music. It is logical as counterpoint, emotional as harmony, balanced as rhythm." (Irvine 324) Set in the ambulatory of Rheims Cathedral after the Dauphin's coronation as Charles VII, it marks the beginning of Joan's fatal isolation from her allies and enemies.

Newton conveyed a sense of her displacement by his blocking. Joan entered stage left* (*Throughout my text, "left" and "right" are from an audience's point of view.) in her glorious new attire to organ music, and then knelt in prayer. This was her first private religious moment in the play and, appropriately, she was alone, except for Dunois and his page off to the top step stage right. Newton's soundscape was punctuation for important passages, and a braiding with the rhetorical orchestration of the scene. On Dunois' paternal "poor innocent child of God" there was a flourish in the background, and when Joan singled him out as her only friend among the nobles, there was more music. "The world is too wicked for me," she lamented, and on her prediction that the French themselves would make an end of her, the musical notes sounded again as underlining, as it were.

Joan's purity and simplicity of faith are pronounced in this scene, especially as she explains her "voices" to Dunois, resorting to a virtually onomatopoeic imitation of their chimes. For this, McLellan had upstage centre where she knelt on the steps. Gone was the earlier emphatic notion of the suffragette or freedom-fighter. This was the simple saint, detached for the moment from the mundane. McLellan's phrasing of the "voices" speech was touching in its projection of her naive faith. There was no question that this Joan believed in her "voices." The only question was whether her belief was once again more reminiscent of children's belief in fairies (as in *Peter Pan*) than in a saint's blurring of hallucination with reality. Instead of having a rapt reverie, we had a charming angelism, though hardly a preparation for the lyrical ecstasy to come.

In almost immediate counterpoint was the processional entrance of Charles, Archbishop, and courtiers, allowing the background music to build an expectation of pomp and ceremony, yet delivering only the extravagances of foolish costumes. Gone was the eroded mediaeval statue look of Chartres - Porteous' artistic reference for the earlier scenes. Now that the French had waxed rich from a collaboration with the English for Joan's captivity, they had turned *nouveau riche* with decadent flamboyance and absurd tastelessness. Lamberts' King had a long blue train with gold *fleurs de lys*, a large coronation cap, and so much gilt and so many adornings (especially around his neck and right arm) that his complaint about "the weight of these robes" was perfectly and comically justified. Unfortunately, Lamberts' persistence on comic neurosis - in the halting, fitful speech and sometimes stumbling movement - did not create the spirit needed to play opposite Joan's increasing melancholy. Joan was obscured in the pomp of the court's entrance, but reasserted herself with bold forthrightness, astonishing her enemies yet again by her rectitude and vehemence. Charles now had no further use of her and was afraid that her continuing presence at court and on the ramparts would prolong the war with England.

Deserted by him, his court, and the Church, she was streaked with a fatalism, rising to angry pride, then sinking into a melancholy bewilderment over the first direct clash with the Archbishop. Outside among the populace, she was an idol, but as the prelate reminded her "You will be none the less alone: they cannot save you." At this moment on stage, McLellan moved downstage right, directly opposite Charles. Her volume increased on "Where would you all have been now if I had needed that sort of truth? There is no help, no counsel, in any of you." She turned to face the audience on "I have always been alone," then turned and ran to Charles and up to Dunois, yelling out her theme in angry defiance, returning downstage and facing the audience again for "I see now that the loneliness of God is His strength...," then collecting herself for a crescendo of defiance and self-assertion, she turned upstage to the Archbishop for her ringingly heroic "I will dare, and dare, and dare, until I die."

Once again she was left visually on the edge of the total stage picture, a way of establishing the point that she was merely one helpless individual against an entire order she did not comprehend. After she ran off to the ovation of the invisible offstage crowd, the ensemble exited in sequence, beginning with Bluebeard - perhaps the most trivial character on stage - and continuing with Dunois, La Hire, and others, followed by the Archbishop and his attendants. Charles was the last to leave, after looking off dispiritedly to stage left. "If only she would keep quiet," he muttered plaintively, "or go home!"

For the final scene of the play proper, McLellan's Joan was once again in the background while all the preparatory talk proceeded on questions of the court's constitution and the nature of the inquisition. This was Shaw's satire on the inner workings of the ecclesiastical court, where personal prejudices of certain members entered into play. Everyone was seated for the preliminaries, with the Inquisitor repeating themes of heresy and Protestantism. Joan was led in through the centre opening of the set. However, McLellan did not indicate any significant physical or mental changes in the character who normally reveals a profound exhaustion or suffering. McLellan raved about the bad fish Joan is served, and was permitted to touch both Cauchon and the Inquisitor before being seated downstage left. She was still self-assured, and her voice as yet strong and hard. Her swift changes in emotional gear - a scornful laugh at D'Estivet's charge regarding her intercourse with evil spirits; a mercurial running from side to side for the passage about her male attire; her bewildered cry "I cannot understand"; her weeping when confronted with the real prospect of death; her despair over being betrayed by her "voices" - did build a dynamic portrait before the crucial recantation and reversal.

Up to the recantation, the merit in McLellan's interpretation was the emphasis on Joan's pride and the blotting out of frailty. So when Joan's faith was broken, and she fell to her knees before the Inquisitor (played with wild irony by Herb Foster), there was a glimpse of vulnerability, though this weakness was connected more to her bitter disillusionment over her "voices" than to the very human recoiling from cruel execution. In this regard, McLellan failed to illuminate the spiritual crux of Joan's problem, and when confronted with the possibility of lifelong incarceration, her lyric despair and tearing-up of the recantation ("Light your fire!") was begun quietly, and turned into a deliberate, self-conscious prose-poem of desire rather than of bitterness. McLellan ignored a possible climax on "My voices were right....they told me you were fools," and went, instead, for a centrestage crescendo on "his ways are not your ways!" after a commotion in the court. Then she turned very quiet for "You are not fit that I shall live among you," stressing a bitter scorn rather than a saintly transcendental peace.

Newton's direction of the ending was marked by pauses, these stretches projecting eerie suspense through Cauchon and the Inquisitor's discussion of the politics of the trial's outcome. De Stogumber's hysterical raving about the horror of Joan's burning changed the mood. Barry MacGregor's gibbering hysteria lost some of the lines, and given that Shaw did not adequately build up the horror of the offstage execution, the moment was reduced even more in performance. Visually, however, the ending had a stark ghastliness with Warwick ascending to the highest part of the risers for his final lines with the Executioner who reports the miracle of Joan's uncremated heart. The slow fade on Warwick's wry "The last of her? Hm! I wonder" was the final note for a tragedy, as well as an intimation of an anti-climactic epilogue.

The Epilogue, which Newton was forced to perform, has always raised problems in terms of its relation to the rest of the play. In a superficial sense it is most obviously comic, for here Shaw plays the part of God laughing at the saint's enemies and murderers. Shaw returns in certain ways to the pantomime conventions of the first two scenes by writing the Epilogue in a deliberately non-realistic mode, turning it into what is probably Joan's own dream in which the living, the dead, and the future are participants. Margery Morgan views the Epilogue as "Shaw's instrument to extend the story of Joan beyond the apparent finality of her death at the stake to a Resurrection and Ascension. Indeed his conformation of her legend to the central myth and ritual of Christianity is made remarkably complete, though the manner of it is condensed and allusive." (Morgan 249) Morgan sees the Harrowing of Hell in the soldier's parole, and interprets De Stogumber's lack of imagination along the lines of a doubting Thomas. She indicates that the décor of Charles' bedchamber - with its candles, yellow and red tapestries, and blowing wind - suggests not only "the *auto-da-fé* which was not actually presented on stage," but "the scene of the Pentecost, the coming of the Holy Ghost in tongues of flame and a rushing mightly wind." (Morgan 249)

The dream sequence has a distinct comic eschatology, with the soldier facetiously describing Hell as a most convivial place: "Like as if you were always drunk without the trouble and expense of drinking. Tip top company too: emperors and popes and kings and all sorts." (Bloom C 131)

Richly suggestive as the Epilogue may be, is it really necessary? Charles A. Berst argues that it is "to show that Joan's history did not end with her martyrdom, but truly began with it." (Berst 290) He recognizes that the Epilogue is a primarily comic pastiche, "serving to offset the grim clouds of the preceding scenes with a more dispassionate perspective." He argues that the Epilogue effects a broad symbolic resolution for the interrelationship between the "tragicomic nature of man and the supernatural nature of Joan." Berst expounds:

> Most notably, the Epilogue dramatically refutes any comfortable notion that *now* man is spiritually more enlightened than were Joan's contemporaries....by Canonizing and by erecting statues man sterilizes and crystallizes his saints, complimenting himself that in freezing them as symbols he is both paying proper homage and revealing his own state of grace. To the contrary, he thus by and large puts his saints out of the way through converting them to his own terms....Modern man, like medieval man,

glories in his dead Joans who, were they living, might well upset his self-esteem, contradict his values, and endanger the status quo. In this light Shaw opens and closes the Epilogue with the rhetorical proposition of Joan's actual resurrection, a proposition followed by man's inevitable response. (Berst 290-291)

This response is that man can accept his Joans in spirit ("where he can pay lip service to them as an ideal"), so long as he does not have to live with them. So as the characters slink away with muttered apologies, Joan is left as isolated as she was in the cathedral and trial scenes.

There is an inescapable sadness about the Epilogue, particularly in Joan's final lines ("O God that madest this beautiful earth, when will it be ready to receive Thy saints? How long, O Lord, how long?"). The Viennese actress Elisabeth Bergner, who played Joan in Max Reinhardt's 1924 production in Berlin before also playing her in English at the Malvern Festival in 1938, commented: "This is the sadness: she is dead and knows more about life than she did before. You mustn't forget, here speaks Joan who isn't alive any more and doesn't judge anymore her own time and what happened. Here speaks a Joan who is above it all." (Hill 4) Or, as Joan Plowright observed, "You do have to suppose that there is a huge difference from the struggle as a mortal being when she comes back as whatever she is. You have to try and suggest some kind of serenity which still encompasses her humour, her background, her struggles, her relationships, but now they are seen from a distance." (Hill 112)

The whole issue of the tone and nature of the Epilogue became strictly academic, however, in Newton's production, for the sequence was staged as a thing completely apart from the rest, with the actors reading their parts at lecterns. This casual presentation offended some audience members, and a local citizen of Niagara accused Newton and his actors of "a lack of zest": For the company to meekly read Shaw's Epilogue to Saint Joan [*sic*], standing behind desks like construing [*sic*] schoolboys about to be flogged for idleness, is an incomprehensible shirking of one of the greatest challenges given to theatrical troupes." (*Niagara Advance*) But as if in final revenge against his detractors, Newton even resisted a taping of the Epilogue when it came time to record his production for archival purposes! When I questioned him recently on whether he had second thoughts about his view of the Epilogue, his response was: "I still don't know whether I'm right. Now that I trust Shaw so much more, I have no answer on that one."

CHAPTER FIVE

HEARTBREAK HOUSE

Newton's 1985 production of *Heartbreak House* seemed like a perfect invitation to renewed controversy, not simply because of its Chekhovian undertones but because of its subtlety as high reasoning satire that sometimes defeated a few of its key players. Shaw claimed to have written "a Fantasy in the Russian manner on English themes," but, as Desmond MacCarthy observed shrewdly, the essential difference between Shaw and Chekhov is one of temperament: "Mr. Shaw does not know what heartbreak is. He conceives it as a sudden disillusionment (vide his heroine), cauterising like a flash of lightning; as a sharp pain, but not as a maiming misery." (MacCarthy 144) Moreover, asserted MacCarthy, Shaw's characters are vital and restless, whereas Chekhov's "are like dying flies in a glue-pot." To make the Chekhovian comparison even more problematic, Shaw "presents his play as an important diagnosis of real conditions, yet he allows his high spirits continually to turn it into farce, so that hardly one person in a hundred sees its relations to reality." (MacCarthy 144)

If the Chekhovian connection is admitted, the director then has to integrate Chekhov's tragicomic manner with Shaw's comedy, though the first problem is for him to decide whether this comedy is farce or high satire. In reviewing the 1920 Theatre Guild production, Alexander Woolcott called the play "quite the larkiest and most amusing one that Shaw has written in many a year" - almost as if it anticipated one of the Aldwych farces of Ben Travers. (Beckerman and Siegman 14) When

Keith Garebian
70

Harold Clurman directed the play in New York in the 1959-60 season (with Maurice Evans, Pamela Brown, Sam Levene, Diana Wynyard. Diane Cilento, and Dennis Price in the cast), he discounted Shaw's remarks about the play's connections with Chekhov. Acknowledging that the title signifies in Shaw's words "cultured, leisured Europe before the (First World) War" and that Chekhov's plays deal with "the educated middle class of the late nineteenth century," before Russia heaved toward revolution, and recognizing, too, that Chekhov's plays - despite their melancholy - are "construed as comedies," Clurman saw the play as utterly un-Chekhovian in style. "Shaw's play is extravagant, full of capering humour which verges on the farcical...Shaw's characters are puppets - unnatural only in the sense that they reveal the truth about themselves more directly, more pointedly, more eloquently, more wittily than people in life are able to." (Smith 415) For his Broadway production, Clurman stressed "a bright-minded whackiness. A puppet show!" taking as his cue Shaw's jokes about bowings, introductions, greetings, et cetera. (Smith 407) Clurman saw the Shotover house as "a loony world," which the characters are expected to take seriously but can't. "As they progress, they become aware of the need to act mad in order to approximate reality." (Smith 408) In Clurman's interpretation the characters were un-English in their behaviour - or more Irish than English because "more impish, more extrovert, more devilish, devilishly comic." The intelligence and ideas in the play were rendered as clowning, with characters "flying off the handle: the 'handle' being the old steady values, the desire to get the hell out of a situation which no longer supports anybody." (Smith 409) Clurman encouraged his players to adopt elements of *opéra-bouffe*, and the "slight duality - a sort of 'gayed up' seriousness - part game, part prophecy" was conceived as "only a reflection of the text itself which begins as a comedy of mad manners and ends with an air raid by an enemy never named or even hinted at throughout the course of the play." (Smith 415-416)

Val Gielgud's celebrated Shaw Festival production in 1968 (with Jessica Tandy, Frances Hyland, Tony van Bridge, and Paxton Whitehead) was closer to a latter-day Restoration comedy than to Clurman's whacky farce. Herbert Whittaker zestfully applauded the Restoration character types: "two ladies of high fashion, two talkative fops, one country maid (who is also Shaw's New Woman as a Young Girl), a gross merchant, a timid philosopher, a snivelling rogue, a maidservant and a prophet." (Bryden 134) In all this zestfulness, Gielgud's production lacked not only the Chekhovian elements but a high poetic line as well, though van Bridge's Shotover, a fiercely irascible patriarch, attained an apocalyptic grandeur and intensity that is all too rarely seen in modern Shavian interpretations, and the production was generally a sophisticated success.

Seventeen years later, Christopher Newton had a fresh vision for the play, reaffirming Shaw's connection with Chekhov, but stressing a surreal element that transcended Chekhov and made a deeper artifice. Although I believe that there are crucial stylistic and temperamental distinctions between Chekhov and Shaw, I am won over to Newton's vision.

Design put an extraordinary stamp on the production. Taking as his cue Nurse Guinness' line, "this house is full of surprises," Michael Levine created an antiquarian mansion capable of growing or shrinking like a dream. With its tall beige walls and picture windows, this was clearly an abode for a cultured, leisured class, but the dusty piles of old papers, scrolls, books, tea-cups, green lamps, and model ships that lay profusely scattered about suggested (as Shaw himself wanted) "a house in which Europe was stifling its soul." Tradition (following Shaw's stage directions) has it that *Heartbreak House* is set in a room resembling part of "an old-fashioned high-pooped ship with a stern gallery." Captain Shotover, after all, thinks of the house as a ship, and Shaw himself obviously intends England to be the ship of state floundering on stormy political and moral seas. However, as is his wont, Christopher Newton forced us to adjust our attitudes to the play by creating a novel opening image - a symbolic framework, as it were, for his probing of the text.

The curtain rose on a penumbral gloom. The piled papers and books looked like spectral stalagmites in a wide, shadowy cave. Dim figures could be seen moving in the background outdoors as a young woman scurried in vain to get their attention. The only sound that was heard was one of gardeners clipping hedges and shrubs on the estate. The young lady, ignored by the servants, settled down with a book on a comfortable chair but then fell asleep, while the rear walls, shuttered windows, and central doorway grew magically as if in some child's fable - *Alice in Wonderland*, perhaps - and the strangeness was compounded by Shotover's first appearance as a wild old bearded man, looking oddly like a combination of "old salt" and *muzhik*, linking English and Russian elements in his appearance. Nurse Guinness' clinking entrance - the result of her teacups on a tray and the shock of discovering the young lady - compounded the mood of something bizarre and unsettling. This was, indeed a house of surprises.

Newton very clearly saw the text as a dream-play, with connections to Strindberg in addition to Chekhov. In his Author's Note for *A Dream Play*, Strindberg wrote: "Time and space do not exist. On a slight groundwork of reality, imagination spins and weaves new patterns made up of memories, experiences, unfettered fancies, absurdities and improvisations. The characters are split, double and multiply; they evaporate, crystallise, scatter and converge. But a single consciousness holds sway over them - that of the dreamer. For him there are no secrets, no incongruities, no scruples and no law....Sleep, the liberator, often appears as a torturer, but when the pain is at its worst, the sufferer awakes - and is thus reconciled with reality." (Strindberg 193)

The overall shape of Newton's production - especially in Jeffrey Dallas' lighting design - appeared to give palpable support to a view of the play as one "of the night, reigned over by the triple Hecate." (Morgan 200) Newton began each act in either deep shadow or darkness, and although there was nocturnal beauty in the final act, the only moon was in a circular window of the outdoor deck. As Morgan asserts: "There can be no natural moon, as Heartbreak House itself, at once strange and familiar, is the underworld of dreams and symbols. Its people have an immensity, a grotesqueness, a symbolic resonance that make them comparable to Blake's mythopoetic images, whose cosmic relevance similarly includes a pointed political allegory." (Morgan 200-201)

The dominant colours were beige, white, and black. Shotover's tan makeup and old clothes, evoking his salt-beaten marine career and sojourn in the tropics, were part of the mixture. Hector looked like a dandy in black, but the servants were in white sailor costumes, and the women - particularly Ellie Dunn and Hesione Hushabye - were contrasting figures in white and black. Ellie was to exert a benevolent white magic over Shotover, while Hesione, with her luxuriant black hair looking like a witch's hood, acted like a vampire or androgynous demon in her black cutaway.

The first movement in the dialogue was marked by Shotover's eccentric talk and behaviour, a point well made by Douglas Rain, an actor who carves a role as if working intricately on a small ivory. With a voice perfectly adapted to careful phrasings and modest tropes of inflection, Rain's Shotover established himself as an old man quite out of the usual run of things or mundane concerns. Shotover is so detached, so preoccupied with his own attempt to attain "the seventh degree of concentration," that he ignores visitors to the house and fails to recognize his own daughter Ariadne. In some ways, of course, he is out of himself, an unreal feeling already presaged by the dreamlike expansion of the house during Ellie's sleep.

The sound changed with Fiona Reid's entrance as Lady Utterword, the fine lady of Horseback Hall. A strikingly trim and brisk figure in her dress and manner, she made us wonder if her bright chatter with throwaway wit was a cultivated manner to protect her psychic hollowness or merely an affectation. Reid, who excels in drawing-room comedy, was titillation plus elegance. Her bird-like flutteriness and lightness of voice, with elegantly inflected irony, contrasted with Goldie Semple's plummy richness as Hesione, and made a fine music - though Newton's production in general was not as intent on vocal rhapsodies as it was on intelligent phrasings and subtextual nuances.

One of the strongest conflicts in the play is that between dream and reality, or between romantic idealism and pragmatic realism. Instead of forcing Ellie and Shotover to one side so that the two sisters could have centre stage for their duologues, Newton maintained an almost equal distribution of focus. Ellie, the sweet young ingénue, was more than a nice young thing in Marti Maraden's performance, combining an eagerness to explore new situations with an inner strength to deal with heartbreak and exalting excitement. Her wide-eyed confrontations with dreamers such as Shotover (with his rum-soaked wisdom) and Hector, and with realists such as Ariadne and Boss Mangan educate her in this strange world. It is through her that Shaw introduces the *leitmotifs* of love and money, for she is about to be married to "a perfect hog of a millionaire for the sake of her father, who is as poor as a church mouse." This father called Mazzini (after a revolutionary soldier and freedom-fighter) is consistently mistaken by Shotover for a pirate rogue and murderer, though Mazzini has struggled consistently to support his family, learning disillusionment in the process of discovering that his poetic paternal grandparents had given him noble ideas but no real profession.

Mazzini's foil is Boss Mangan, the "Napoleon of industry" who once gave him a gift of capital, knowing full well that this money would eventually ruin Mazzini. Unfortunately, Allan Gray's Mazzini was an inadequate counterpoint to Robert Benson's boringly confident Mangan, because he missed many notes in his interpretation of the ineffectual intellectual. Gray, who is normally the right actor to be smilingly ingratiating and obliging, did not project a sweet zaniness. His taupe costume was the only statement of his humbled position, and his acting showed no convincing awe at the world of surprises, no humility from within.

Where Mangan and Mazzini are realists - or are forced to be this by circumstances - Ellie is the young dreamer who moves from dreamy bewilderment to tough, calculating strength. She is infatuated with Marcus Darnley, and when she discovers that he is none other than Hesione's husband in a long black coat and dandified hat, she is embarrassed at her own gullibility. This is her first heartbreak, though, as she remarks to Hesione (who has taken Hector's "affair" in cool stride): "I have a horrible fear that my heart is broken, but that heartbreak is not like what I thought it must be." This, indeed, might well be Shaw's shrewd anticipation of a critical objection that he does not really understand the nature of true heartbreak. Hesione's response is Shaw's own view of the subject ("It's only life educating you, pettikins"), for as he made clear to his Austrian writer-friend Siegfried Trebitsch, "heartbreak" meant a "chronic complaint, not a sudden shock." (Smith 420)

Much of the fun and force of Act I derive from the interplay of the sisters, and the contrast between Goldie Semple and Fiona Reid brought this interplay vividly to life. Newton showed Hesione's physical and psychological dominance of Ellie and others by positioning her at the apex of an imaginary triangle in the blocking, with Ellie and Mangan or Ariadne at opposite corners downstage. Levine's exquisite costuming emphasized the slenderness and height of the actresses, but the androgynous elements in Hesione's costume added a masculine virility and aggressiveness to her stage picture in striking contrast to Fiona Reid's stylishly conventional Ariadne. Semple made much of Hesione's *hauteur* and of her relish over the power to "fascinate" men, but she did not neglect the character's banal mind.

At the opposite pole was Reid's Ariadne, a crafty, sleek vixen, rampant with lubricious *double-entendres* that invite Hector's lady-killing response like something out of Congreve or Wilde. This exchange was wonderfully effective on stage - more because of Reid than because of Norman Browning's strained and stentorian Hector - and Reid's Ariadne emerged with her true "spine," that is, an essentially hollow playfulness that could be "accursedly attractive" to Hector, while being empty of heartfelt passion. Ariadne plays at devotion and heartbreak; she does not have a heart to break. If she does, it is left at Horseback Hall.

Men, especially husbands, are clearly the "damned creatures" in Act I. They fall prey to women's romantic designs. The women are demons: Shotover points out that Hesione has used up Hector like a vampire sucking the life-blood out of its victim; Ariadne, as Hector himself admits, has "claws" and "the diabolical family fascination"; and Ellie, who had managed to charm Shotover from their first meeting, is called "little devil" admiringly by Hesione. Against these creatures, the men have little chance. Hector is forced to wear whatever costume Hesione decrees, and the only battle he wins is a purely imaginary one with an imaginary opponent whom he duels for the hand of an imaginary woman. Randall yearns after Ariadne, but he is a nearly hysterical baby, while she is completely unruffled in her narcissism. And Mangan, though nearer to reality than either Hector or Randall, discovers that Ellie has a practical wisdom beyond her young years.

The first act underlined the "magic" in the characters, suggesting that Ellie's benevolent or "white" magic was offset by Hesione's destructive "black" magic, and that Shotover's own "magic" - achieved out of his rum, labour, and hard knocks in life - will get at some primal reality that will sweep away the muddled world's anarchic forces. In this regard, the conclusion of Act I was directed as a sort of ritual, combining Chekhovian, biblical, and classical themes. The scene was carried to a swelling, quasi-mystical crescendo after a brief but intense discussion between Shotover and Hector on the powers of life and death. Hesione entered and shifted the conversation back to the subjects of superstition and money. The dream mood, which had opened the act, redeveloped curiously - this time from an antiphonal chant by the three characters left on stage - and the act concluded ceremoniously and strangely. The personal dimension, which Newton had established with his opening focus on Ellie's dream, was displaced by the group chant which culminated in Shotover's appeal for "deeper darkness" in which money and destruction could be made.

Act II extended the dream feeling. The huge room started in darkness as light was let in by a single shaft through the hallway stage right. Then once the servants (still dressed as sailors) opened the centre door, the light came up strongly. In this act Newton once again emphasized the women as magical characters who had men at their mercy, and now it was time for Mangan's heartbreak. Ellie was seen as a pragmatist, quite able to say the most deflating things with perfectly sweet frankness and plainness. She dealt firmly but kindly with Mangan: "It's no use pretending that we are Romeo and Juliet. But we can get on very well together if we choose to make the best of it." Mangan loves her, but she loves Hector, and he becomes exasperated by this "crazy house," accusing Ellie of hypnotic power, for she has been able to get him to admit that he had deliberately ruined Mazzini, and she will now rub his forehead and put him to sleep as in a spell.

Newton maintained the interplay of dark and light - literally in the stage lighting and metaphorically in the character relationships. The Nurse's simulated ballet in the dark to piano music drifting in from the hallway off stage right was a curious duality of reality and phantasmagoria. Tripping over Mangan in the dark, she was frightened by the suggestion that he might be dead. Much of the subsequent dialogue and action occurred during this phase of Mangan's "unconsciousness," and Newton retained his pattern of triangular blocking. Both corners of an imaginary triangle had been used for sleep - the downstage left side in Act I for Ellie's dozing-off, and the right one for Mangan's "spell." The apex of this imaginary triangle lay in the tall, narrow doorway near centre, which was often given to Hesione so that her dramatic black form could be set off by the yellow light of the doorway. This positioning was particularly effective for her tirade against Mazzini Dunn for letting Ellie become engaged to Mangan. Here Goldie Semple's black hair and cutaway completed the image of a witch.

Mangan's sleeping form became an occasion of comedy, for in her flirtation with Mazzini, Hesione had to lean across the burly one's body. In the process of her attempted charming of Mazzini, Mangan's body slumped off his chair to the floor, but Hesione and Mazzini continued their conversation unperturbed by this.

The duologue between Hesione and Ellie proceeded with Ellie portraying herself as someone in hell, though with a consoling pragmatism ("Well, if I can't have love, that's no reason why I should have poverty"). Now she had become one of what Hesione called "impudent little fiends," fully aware that she was buying Mangan. Sexual tension bristled in this duologue because of Ellie's yearning for Hector whom, she claims, she would have made into a man and not simply "a household pet" as Hesione had done. "Oh, what right had you to take him all for yourself!" Marti Maraden's Ellie cried in anguish, showing yet another manifestation of her heartbreak. This was the tense scene in which the image of hair represented special energy, a higher force and *élan vital* linked with the will to succeed:

MRS HUSHABYE. What would you say if I were to box your ears?

ELLIE [calmly] I should pull your hair.

MRS HUSHABYE [mischievously] That wouldnt hurt me. Perhaps it comes off at night.

ELLIE [so taken aback] Oh, you dont mean to say, Hesione, that your beautiful black hair is false?

MRS HUSHABYE [patting it] Dont tell Hector. He believes in it.

ELLIE [groaning] Oh! Even the hair that ensnared him false! Everything false!

MRS HUSHABYE. Pull it and try. Other women can snare men in their hair, but I can swing a body on mine. Aha! you cant do that, Goldylocks.

Hesione's black hair reinforces the symbolism of what J.E. Cirlot calls "dark, terrestrial energy," (Cirlot 129) whereas Ellie's "golden" hair (not so represented, however, in Newton's production) is related to the sun's rays. In this production Hesione's spiritual energy was clearly demarcated as being sinister and malevolent, whereas Ellie's power was that of warding off Hesione's negative energy and comforting Shotover.

Newton clearly indicated in this act that the play was about warring forces (Heartbreak House and Horseback Hall) which modulated the action. Dream states could become disagreeable - as when Mangan's hypnotic state leads him to overhear a "shocking" conversation between the ladies. Hesione tries to control the damage by insisting that Mangan has dreamt it all, but Mangan will not be appeased. This becomes yet another moment of heartbreak, for Mangan is now seen as a human being with a real heart.

The Burglar incident (in which Andrew Gillies' tame playing hardly filled the image of a masked sad trickster) carries this neurotic "madness" to a new height and upshot. The Burglar, who reveals his express stratagem to seek his own salvation at the expense of the rich, is Shaw's comic device of fortifying the play's structure by the personal disorder and "games" that tear away at social illusions. The Burglar incident has a bitter undernote in that the others who chastise the felon for his dishonesty are themselves hypocrites who do not reform the system that permits blackmail by both criminal and prosecutors. The inhabitants of Heartbreak House no longer believe in the old justice. The criminal no longer believes in his crime: it is simply another way of earning a living. Billy Dunn (the "drinking Dunn" in contrast to his relative Mazzini, "the thinking Dunn") is a clown or "ham" actor, capable of being momentarily contrite, shrewd, pious, dishonest, jocular - but Andrew Gillies played him as an old eccentric in beard and whiskers, and somewhat diminished the seriocomic scale of the part.

The grotesque revelation that the Burglar happens to be the Nurse's estranged husband is a comic shock, but the tone of this section becomes abstractly spiritual. Newton's blocking used the entire stage, with characters not simply favouring corners or the apex of the imaginary triangle, but actually spreading themselves across the width. The expansiveness of stationing provided a geometry to the spreading heartbreak.

A quasi-Chekhovian calm developed - broken only temporarily by Reid's heartless bustling. Attention focused on Shotover's cool detachment: he was not particularly concerned with the world because, in his age, he was nearly out of it. As he grew increasingly misanthropic (calling Mangan a hog, warning Ellie not to sell her soul, defending his Zanzibar demonism), Ellie sat by him for his speech about the foolishness and corruption of the world. This was not delivered as a radiant aria but as a calm vision, with Rain's narrow vocal range making him an important member of an ensemble rather than an isolated star. This intelligent actor lacked the emotive power to turn Shotover into a rivettingly dominant figure - a slightly dotty Lear mixed with a questionable Prospero - but Rain did not lose his opportunities for clever quips, neat epigrams, or gnomic utterances. His Shotover was Tennysonian rather than Shakespearean or Chekhovian, and without an emotional intimacy.

The act concluded with a scene between Hector and Randall, in which the two were noticeably upset by the air of the house. With Ariadne's entrance, the scene became a fugue in a different key on the theme of demonic dreaminess, with "Randall the Rotter" faltering in his vow to seek revenge on Ariadne for her "most cruel" power over him. Randall turned sleepy, and the curtain descended slowly after Hector's exit with his hands uplifted in an invocation to heaven to fall and crush women. Unfortunately, what should have been a climactic gesture of impotent exasperation became in Norman Browning's fulsomely self-complacent and self-conscious performance merely an histrionic decoration - rather like his exotic Arab costume.

When the curtain arose on Act III, the nautical and dream metaphors were extended by Michael Levine's extraordinary setting. The design was evocative of the sea and a ship's deck, with hedges sculpted to look like wave crests, and the acting area turned into a white plank deck with canvas deck chairs, a white temple-like structure at the rear with tall, columnar doorways and crowned with a triangular shape. There was a circular window set within the triangle and glowing yellow like a full moon, the production's equivalent for Shaw's "moon in its opal globe." The white deck, railings, doorways, and ship's ventilators were set off by the deep black night, and everything seemed suspended in space, as if floating in time. There was a dreaminess in the image, with Ellie and Shotover huddled together downstage right, and with Hesione adding a sinister note by a reference to "a sort of splendid drumming in the sky,"

The black and white colour scheme was maintained in the costuming, with Hesione in black, Ariadne and Ellie in white capes, Shotover in black boots and coat with white trousers, and Hector in long flowing white robes, now more reminiscent of classical Greece than of Arabia. Semple's dark Hesione walked against the background of the white "temple," and reinforced the suggestion of a classical siren. Of course, the associations with Greek tragedy were present, too, in certain of Hector's lines: "Heaven's threatening growl of disgust at us useless creatures...Either out of the darkness some new creation will come to supplant us as we have supplanted the animals, or the heavens will fall in thunder and destroy us."

Gone was any deliberate bitter-sweet Chekhovian feeling. Instead the mood was portentously dreamy, until fragmented by Ariadne's smug bourgeois chatter, a symptom of her Horseback Hall sensibility: "All this house needs to make it a sensible, healthy, pleasant house, with good appetites and sound sleep in it, is horses....There are only two classes in good society in England: the equestrian classes and the neurotic classes. It isn't mere convention: everybody can see that the people who hunt are the right people and the people who dont are the wrong ones.'' Ariadne's prim and very English attitude stands in dramatic contrast to her father's wild, Dionysian sensibility.

The dialogue which ensued about Mangan's income and factories and the desirable sort of government added a satiric colour to the dream world. It followed quite naturally that Ellie would recognize the unreality of the house and its characters, where everything was illusory or delusory. Marcus' tigers were false, as were Mangan's millions. Nothing was real or strong about Hesione except her black hair, and Ariadne's beauty was the only real thing about her, except for the ''mothering tyranny'' that Fiona Reid brought out in her performance.

The Chekhovian connection - especially with *The Cherry Orchard* - was re-established in this section, just as the sounds of some dimly apprehended war broke. As Margery Morgan comments, the suspension of action at this point in the play ''reflects the arrested life of a society about to break up and from its ruin perhaps release the germ of a new order.'' (Morgan 209) Newton, however, resisted the aimless wandering of characters around the set, managing, instead, an interesting arrangement of the ensemble, with Shotover and Ellie huddled together and Ariadne, at a sharp angle to them, looking into the distance. Hesione usually had the background in which to prowl about, but because of her distance away from the others in the ensemble, she could not really dominate the grouping. The first-half of this act had little physical movement, allowing the darker tones of the play to assert themselves with only minimal offstage music and sound effects. The predominant impression was one of stillness, dreamy but not really peaceful, except for Ellie's gentleness with her ''natural captain,'' ''spiritual husband and second father.'' Even Shotover's irony was gentle in his admission that he was happier now for being half-dead.

The spiritual peace of this incongruous couple reinforced the slant of Newton's production - a slant that was given further point by Mazzini's abrupt entrance at the rear, where he stood in his dressing-gown like a timely priest. He entered just before Mangan fumed and then howled about being made a fool by Ellie. This howl indicated a powerful bedevilment precipitating heartbreak, and the heartbreak theme was renewed in Ellie's musical chant about ''this silly house, this strangely happy house, this house without foundations. I shall call it Heartbreak House.'' As Hector added ''We do not live in this house: we haunt it,'' Ariadne spoke of the house's power to draw her back, failing to see the heartbreak she herself had caused for her father. Instead she continued to assert her own peculiar bourgeois attitude which divided existence into two simple categories - one of disorder and untidiness, and the other of healthy appetites and good stables. No wonder she was a Mrs. Utterword, for all she could do was utter mere words without spiritual depth.

"How is this all going to end?" wondered Hector, but Norman Browning's reading fetched laughter at Shaw's apparent formlessness, instead of obtaining nervous laughter at the prospect of a cataclysm. The point of this sequence was that the quasi-Chekhovian stasis (which Mazzini referred to in his line "Nothing ever does happen") was a prelude to a shattering event. As explosions built offstage (including one in Shotover's gravel pit that was stocked with dynamite) and the lights went out, Shotover and Ellie were blasted with a peculiar ecstasy. Mangan and Billy Dunn rushed to their doom, and Ariadne urged a false jingoistic sentiment that echoed a well-known war ballad. Shotover warned that the "ship" (England) would split and sink, and he called for all to stand by "for judgement." Ellie was excited by the thunder which, to her, sounded like Beethoven, and in her intense ecstasy she urged Marcus/Hector to set fire to the house that he had called the "soul's prison." The metaphors of ship and sea, storm and thunder, indicated forces greater than human reasoning. For Ellie and Shotover, now soul-mates, the impending catastrophe led to a release like that of sexual orgasm. But Douglas Rain did not project this intensity sufficiently to support Marti Maraden's Ellie in her gleeful awakening from drowsy peace.

All lights went out briefly as the characters awaited some final explosion. But the cataclysm never came, and they discovered that all had survived, except for Mangan and Billy Dunn. "The ship is safe," proclaimed Shotover. And safe, too, was the enchantment of Heartbreak House. As Hesione invoked the survivors to return the next day - and Ellie echoed the sentiment - we were to see, Newton appeared to be saying, that Heartbreak House itself was an enchanted temple, a site of sirens and men still held captive by glamour and desire.

The final tableau - with Hesione, Shotover, and Mazzini each stationed at a doorway in the background - left us with a strong image of forces reasserted. Ellie once again was isolated, but now her inner strength was such that she was an emblem of dream rounded off in allegory. Her love and acquired wisdom were not to be dismissed, however, as illusory. She was self-absorbed to a high degree, but she had managed to deal with the chaos threatening to destroy all. Yet there was something else in her final image: by remaining by herself downstage, she was emblematic of the splitting of humanity. In other words, the final tableau was an expression of ambivalence. Shaw and Newton had worked in tandem, as it were, to evoke the strange fascination (in Hesione, Ellie, and Shotover) which destroyed moral sense and carried the characters beyond honour and dishonour. Ellie's final radiance (with its key word "hope") demonstrated Shaw's audacity. A purportedly anti-war play invited the audience to a ritualistic mockery of patriotism while, nevertheless, rescuing the characters from final despair. The ghost of Chekhov faded away, but the spectre of Shavian fantasy grew and gleamed.

CHAPTER SIX

MAJOR BARBARA

In his programme note for the 1987 production Newton revealed an allegorical slant:

> The first cue is in the name of the first character. Britomart was the virtuous lady knight in Spencer's *The Fairy Queen* [*sic*]. It's rather like calling a character Lancelot. We know that we should look around for a mythic underpinning somewhere. In this case, we find two quests: in the first we discover an extremely wealthy woman (Britomart) looking for more money; in the second, we see Undershaft's search for an heir. The quests collide. There is a descent into hell (the Salvation Army shelter) and an ascent into an earthly Paradise. The end suggests that Cusins and Barbara will together use the power of Undershaft to make 'war on war.'

Leaving aside a problem in Newton's allegorical slant - Barbara is displaced from the important position she bears in both quests, and is not seen as the principal figure in a third for true faith and mission - we should record that Newton was able to give emblematic resonance to the characters and conflicts and to achieve the parabolic power of the story.

His production opened as a comedy of manners in Lady Britomart's Wilton Crescent Boudoir, with its Turkish chandeliers, fluted columns, heavy lamps, bulbous urns, stained-glass windows, potted ferns, and tiers of unread books. The expensive trappings emphasized a cosy, secure, well-ordered, respectable environment. There was a feminine voluptuousness projected by the curves of urns and lamps and the rich, heavy fabrics reminiscent of what Margery Morgan calls "an atmosphere of womblike security." (Morgan 148) Frances Hyland's Lady Britomart (whose first name is Bridget or "strength") was Shaw's parody of Britannia and of the upper-class matriarch of countless drawing-room comedies - most notably of Lady Bracknell in Oscar Wilde. Hyland, who can act highhandedly imperious with ease, was the very image of unperturbed self-possession, as she commanded her children without patronizing them. The dominant theme in this act is one of money, for Lady Britomart intends to solicit her estranged husband for an increase in financial support, even though she is thoroughly opposed to his ethics, "religion of wrongness," and Machiavellian mode of wielding power.

This act proceeds chiefly by way of conventional interview and cross-examination, with Stephen, who is in awe of his mother, submitting to her coolly aggressive directness of approach and reproach. Hyland emphasized Lady Britomart's materialism rather than her humanity, and the only remarkable points about her as a woman were her quickness to preach indulgence and tolerance of others, while really manipulating situations to her own advantage. Her stylish composure and peremptory candour made the emphases clear: Sarah would have to find at least another £800 a year for the next ten years; Barbara would need at least £2,000 a year; Stephen must marry soon and so something must be arranged for him. Yes, Andrew Undershaft always defended nonsense and wickedness and did everything perverse on principle, but it was not a question of whether to take money from him, but simply a question of how much. She remained ever in control, whether disapproving of Barbara's ability to order others about, or stifling young Lomax's frivolous humour and paroxysms of laughter. The tone turned more diversionary only briefly, with Jim Mezon's quick-spoken Cusins, Barbara Worthy's spirited Sarah, and Michael Howell's silly Lomax, but as soon as Douglas Rain's Undershaft took the scene, the act resumed its paradoxical course as a gravely witty satire.

Rain's Undershaft was an easygoing, kindly, patient man with a watchful waiting face. The comedy of his poor memory of his own children was effected by the actor's practised gentleness and delicate shyness, and it was left to Mezon's Cusins to introduce the father to his own children. Rain compounded the comedy by his formal politeness and silence, indicating the character's inability to relax with his own family. Here, undoubtedly, was a stranger in their midst - a stranger with a strange point of view about life. It was not long, however, before Undershaft warmed to his own paradoxes, turning amiable about his firm's progress with armaments, scoffing at peace on earth and goodwill to men, and gilding his shamelessness with elegant poise. The actor's silken grace was superb, though it was questionable whether Rain could call on latent reserves of power for Undershaft's Dionysian energy and charisma.

The play introduces two divergent religions - Undershaft's devilish unorthodoxy and Barbara's Christian Salvationism, each the extreme of the other. Undershaft is Nietzschean in his shock tactics of striking at the very essence of Christian philosophy and theology with his exploitative energy and irony. The shadow of Dionysus falls across many of his lines. Like the wild god, he has, he reports, a ''natural talent for stepdancing,'' and like Dionysus, he associates himself with loud music. With a hint of Dionysus' violence, he claims to be ''a profiteer in mutilation and murder,'' rejoicing in the explosion of twenty-seven dummy soldiers by an experimental gun at the foundry. Where his daughter's symbol is the cross, his is the sword; where her motto is salvation by the blood of the Lamb and the fire of the Holy Sprit, his is Blood and Fire of destruction and death.

The play becomes a contest for souls, rather than one for money alone, although it is money that is a potent sacramental in this intense struggle. Undershaft lays the ground for his eventual victory over Barbara by getting her to agree to his bargain: he will visit her Salvation shelter if she will visit him the next day in his cannon works. When the two shake hands at the bargain, the good grace of the proceedings harmonizes with poised irony. Lady Britomart scolds: ''Really, Barbara, you go on as if religion were a pleasant subject. Do have some sense of propriety.'' Then she asks Charles Lomax to ring for prayers. All this after the heavy discussion about finances! The act concludes with the sound of hymn singing in the background, as all but Undershaft (who has already left) and Stephen (who tries to play the rebel) go in to worship in a spirit of the church militant. The final image of this act is, as Robert G. Everding contends, ''The antithesis of the scene's beginning one,'' because ''There is no longer harmony between the person and the environment,'' and the library ''is no longer the centre of meaningful activities; it is now a retreat from a more vital existence that thrives beyond the confines of the library.'' The final stage picture is that of a young man ''isolated from society and clinging stubbornly to his conventional morality.'' (Leary 110)

Newton's production achieved this picture splendidly. Lady Britomart's boudoir now seemed more claustrophobic than cosy, with the large window covered against the cold night air, and the overbearing presence of books now completing the image of ''a closed-minded world that locks out reality and defends its own ethic, an ideological as well as physical prison for the people who inhabit it.'' (Leary 110)

Act I is the shortest section of the play. The second act matches the third in being the longest, in terms of text. It was set by Cameron Porteous in a huge, cold, noisy courtyard, rattled by the echo of passing trains overhead. Shaw's script calls for a building that is "newly whitewashed," for the whitewash in what is a grotesque setting "covers over the essential reality of the slum warehouse just as the Salvation Army's religious fervour conceals its political value to the rich. This warehouse is in truth as much a part of the commercial world as the grimy warehouses in the background." (Leary 111) Porteous' design did not adhere strictly to the text - it had the suggestion of whitewash by a bucket and brush - but achieved a fine sense of purgatory with the steam from soup pots and passing trains, and the general black and grey griminess.

Newton introduced this section with a long, wordless silence, before Snobby Price's entrance. The Cockney lowlifers were a Dickensian underworld of bullying menace, lying exploitation, and weak or fey subjection. The heavy use of demotic argot in distorted accents was a sign of dehumanization. We clearly had vices on parade: pride, anger, lying, ignorance, jealousy, malice, despair, vengeance. Irene Hogan's diminutive but stocky Rummy Mitchens (in cap and moth-eaten cape), and Helen Taylor's Jenny Hill, a meek Salvation lass, were the feminine form of Crosstianity (the religion of suffering submission), while Ted Dykstra's swaggering Snobby Price and Jon Bryden's hulking Bill Walker (a version of Sykes) formed a demonic, masculine force, with Herb Foster's half-worn, half-hardened Peter Shirley standing apart by his bristling disdain for those who accept the indignity of poverty and deprivation.

Martha Burns' Barbara was herself an ironic form of Crosstianity, having mistaken the superficial forms of faith and love for a true inward grace. Shaw's heroine does not see through the fraudulence of her mission poor, who are more than willing to pretend a conversion in return for food, shelter, and money. Barbara is too naive to recognize the burlesquing of Christianity by Snobby and Rummy, just as she is too zealous to see that her gospel of submission is really a message of defeat, for it accepts poverty as a test of faith rather than as an unnecessary evil. She is an analogue of Christ, but her insistent denial of the possibility of evil in human nature renders her vulnerable to her father's Mephisthophelean stratagem to woo her soul. Undershaft knows that the root cause of much evil is the crime of poverty. The second act is Barbara's process of disillusionment and spiritual devastation.

The Cockney lowlifers are demons of conniving greed, theft, and violence. As such they fit in appropriately with the West Ham Shelter which, to Andrew Undershaft, is a hell that he can harrow in order to win his daughter and, ironically, rescue her from her naive theology. This is an act in which the Dionysian references crystallize dramatically - especially around the figures of Undershaft and Cusins - and in which Barbara's relationship to Christ is tested before an apocalyptic transfiguration. It is distinctly an act that substantiates William G. McCollom's contention that the play "contains a plot within an allegory." (Bloom A 37) The question is what will win - Undershaft's money and gunpowder or Barbara's faith and charity? This section of the play is filled with various climaxes - Cusins' noisy mischief with rhetoric and drum, Undershaft's towering intensity, and, most importantly, Barbara's disillusionment and subsequent transfiguration.

Shaw manages a voluptuous rhetoric within the passion, but the difficulty for a director is in finding players who can encompass this passion and voluptuousness without appearing to be vulgarly melodramatic or absurd. Shaw compounds the director's problem by balancing comedy across the tightrope of tragedy. None of his three principals - Barbara, Undershaft, or Cusins - is without moments of mischief or gay levity. Barbara cracks Salvation Army jokes and snatches a kiss from Cusins across his huge drum. Though marked by high, forceful energy (Shaw describes him with participles such as "surging," "seizing," "pressing," "pushing"), Undershaft cracks witty paradoxes and turns his discussions into a farce of rationalization. Cusins becomes a Dionysian devotee with his drinking, drumming, singing, and declaiming.

Shaw here is actually incarnating ecstasy, but Newton's production fell a little short in this regard, despite largely excellent performances from his ensemble and principal players. Jim Mezon was, perhaps, the most successful of the three principals in registering the pitch that the script requires, especially in his drumming on the stoop in honour of Bodger, the distiller-philanthropist who turns out to be Lord Saxmundham. Mezon's propensity for gleeful physical abandon and rapid speech certainly created a high energy, though even this actor lacked a thundering flourish. Douglas Rain's Undershaft scored fine points in the subtle details of his role, as he sat patiently off to one side, alertly observing others, before launching into his gospel. As far as Undershaft's watchful gravity, cool confidence, grim sympathy, and triumphant concentration were concerned, Rain had no difficulty in showing a formidable core beneath an easy-going surface. What he lacked was the temperament of an ecstatic devil. It was a matter of scale in the passion and excitement, as well as a question of vocal quality. Rain's voice is best suited to a middle range. It admits of numerous subtle shadings of inflection and rhythm, but it seems to be incapable of the grand line or of storm and stress. Rain is a witty actor rather than a mighty one. Undershaft the Socialist evangelist, Undershaft the estranged paterfamilias, and Undershaft the crafty soul-seducer were all within the actor's range; but Undershaft the towering Nietzschean or Dionysian hero was not. No matter how much Rain redoubled his force with certain lines or attempted a sardonic energy, the character never took on anything that transcended the limits of an infernal old rascal of graceful manners and a soothing voice.

This left most of the ecstasy to Martha Burns' Barbara, but the actress, although intelligent and humane in her portrayal of the heroine's ministry, betrayal, and abandonment, could not reach the quick of agony. Shaw complicates the role by first making her seem brisk and businesslike at the shelter, disarmingly sincere in her faith, and complacent to the point of blandness. She is a wooing angel, eager to teach that man cannot serve both God and Mammon. Her gentleness is that of a saint, but the dramatic problem, as with all saints, is how to make goodness seem vital without weakening it by an optimistic passivity. It is a problem that is further magnified by the fact that Cusins and Undershaft have all the cadences to make a full closure in the dialogue, whereas Barbara really has far fewer lines than they. An irony is that as she sets to winning Bill Walker's soul, her father sets to winning hers. And it is the burden of Crosstianity (or even of Christianity) that weighs her down before she is almost broken by her father's devilish cleverness and power. Her great shock is that the Salvation Army rests ultimately on the support of its worst enemies - those, like her father and Bodger, who make the money they donate out of the very misery and degradation that she and the Army fight. She is disillusioned when Mrs. Baines eagerly accepts Bodger's money, and when Cusins joyously celebrates the "unselfishness" of Undershaft and Bodger.

In the critical stages of Barbara's dawning disillusionment, Martha Burns hit high notes of passion. Her fervour on "Two million millions would not be enough" was exemplary, as was her ardour on "No: the Army is not to be bought." But in the deeper stages, when devastation floods her being, this Barbara lacked the full gloom of a once-radiant angel. Newton devised a wonderful context for her moment of agony. After Cusins' Dionysian declaration ("Dionysos Undershaft has descended. I am possessed") and a noisy procession with drum, tambourine, and trombone, to an accompaniment of chugging train sounds, there was a palpable pause. Then Barbara's emotional despair on "Drunkenness and Murder!" led into yet another pause, this time a long one, marked by billowing smoke above the train culvert right on her next line: "My God: why hast thou forsaken me?" Her agitation was given a quasi-mystical significance, and both Burns and Newton managed to downplay the amazing presumptuousness of the character who identifies boldly with Christ on the cross. Burns projected a quiet contemplativeness just prior to her feigned perky excitement as she urged Peter Shirley to tell her all about Paine and Bradlaugh, secularist dissenters. At this moment, she yielded to her ideological antagonists. What was missing, however, was the pathos of Gethsemane. To be fair to the actress, the problem originated in Shaw's script, for Barbara's unique poetic and ironic power is too compressed to offset the preceding climax of Undershaft's joining the Army band. Barbara's isolation at the end of this act does not quite have the theatrical impact of Saint Joan's isolation in Rheims or at the trial.

In the first scene of Act III, back in Wilton Crescent, Barbara is without her Salvation Army uniform for the first time. She is anguished and angry at what her father has done to her, and Burns made a strong point of this wracking passion with her "Do you understand what you have done to me?" before breaking into a weeping condemnation of Undershaft's ruthless exploitation of his victims: "I could forgive you if my forgiveness would open the gates of heaven to you. But to take a human soul from me, and turn it into the soul of a wolf!" The last three words were uttered with enough disgust to vibrate like a curse, but Rain's Undershaft was too strong a force to be subdued in this manner. With Cusins' earlier admission of Undershaft's Dionysian power ("He sat there and completed the wreck of my moral basis, the rout of my convictions, the purchase of my soul"), it was clear that this "Prince of Darkness" could cause not only intoxication and hangover, but could also transfigure human beings so as to inspire them quite beyond themselves. Mezon's acting was deliberately devoid of the conventional traits of drunkenness, so as to suggest that his intoxication the night before was, as Margery Morgan puts it, "spiritual and inspirational, not crudely orgiastic." (Morgan 141) In his subsequent account of the Salvation meeting, Mezon's Cusins provided an amazing version of a transfiguration in which devotees were exalted to a fervour by the "Prince of Darkness."

Shaw does not afford the actress who plays Barbara much help in her struggle against such a formidable foe. The transition from revulsion and condemnation to new-found faith is made almost instantaneously, and not even the very greatest actress could effect such a swift change without difficulty or strained credibility. Shaw very probably wanted to find a way of acting on the bargain between Undershaft and Barbara, and of finding a way to move very quickly from Wilton Crescent to Perivale St. Andrews. On the positive side, Barbara's quick transition and the subsequent scene-change do keep the emphasis on a spiritual contest without ever obscuring the plot-business of determining Undershaft's true spiritual heir.

The Perivale St. Andrews scene materialized by means of a revolve, timed to Cusins' angry "Avaunt!" to Undershaft, and the sound of loudly clanging trains. Because Shaw alludes to vernal April, Porteous put his characters in summer whites (though Undershaft wore a laboratory coat) and pale pastels in order to increase the white look of his décor. Perivale St. Andrews is where Undershaft practises his version of corporate feudalism, and it is described by Shaw as "an almost smokeless town of white walls, roofs of narrow green slates or red tiles, tall trees, domes, campaniles, and slender chimney shafts, beautifully situated and beautiful in itself." Shaw also describes a concrete emplacement, a parapet "which suggests fortification, because there is a huge cannon..." Porteous' set eliminated all clutter, maintaining an almost Grecian look with tall columns(really factory silos), a semi-circular arrangement of steps, and a parapet (dominated by the huge, phallic cannon and the green rooftops of the village beneath the armoury). Three dummy soldiers - one lying across a step - were suggestive of an ironically clean Golgotha, from where Undershaft could view and dominate the world as a battlefield. The set was meant to represent Undershaft's point of view, and the heavy gloss on the floor gave off a cold light and reflection in this clean corporate utopia. The scenic design substantiated Cusins' declaration: "Everything perfect! wonderful! real! It only needs a cathedral to be a heavenly city instead of a hellish one."

Actually, the paradox of a heaven made out of hellish means was amplified only after a musical interlude for the scene change. This was yet another instance of Newton's mode of seducing an audience into accepting his novel conception. The setting completed an allegorical triptych, in which, paradoxically and ironically, Wilton Crescent, the West Ham Shelter, and Perivale St. Andrews were all versions of heaven or hell. For Lady Britomart, the rich, cluttered opulence of Wilton Crescent was obviously a comfortable paradise, though it was rejected by Barbara. For Barbara, the Shelter was a temporal heaven for poor souls who needed daily bread even more desperately than divine bread, yet to Undershaft it was a place of oppressive horror. Similarly, where Undershaft viewed his armoury as a plutocrat's paradise, Barbara was apt to see it as a diabolonian refuge. The play's movement from Lady Britomart's uterine boudoir to Undershaft's utopian city (with Peter Shirley as the newly-appointed gatekeeper and timekeeper) is Shaw's way of emphasizing the mythological unity. Where Lady Britomart dominates Wilton Crescent, and Barbara dominates the West Ham Shelter, it is Undershaft who rules Perivale St. Andrews, and it is he who is apparently poised to win Barbara's soul and Cusins'.

Shaw stacks everything in favour of Undershaft's "religion." Sarah and Stephen, hardly their father's favourites, are thrilled beyond belief at the factory, although in the production, Barbara Worthy's Sarah was startled by one of the dummies that Undershaft kicked out of his way. Cusins is unable to find anything discreditable. And the time is ripe for Undershaft to wax eloquent on the subject of his industrial progress - indeed, on the progress of civilization itself. This scene marks the full extent of Undershaft's realism, and the separate conversions of Cusins and Barbara to a new realism. This is also where the themes of money and Undershaft's heir are resolved.

The first major action is Cusins' confession, in which he reveals that he has abandoned his conscience in favour of his passion for Barbara. The implication is that he is not a true Salvationist, but merely one out of convenience in order to be near his beloved. She is the object of his worship: "Dionysus and all the others are in herself. I adored what was divine in her, and was therefore a true worshipper. But I was romantic about her too." The Dionysian reference establishes one aspect of the play's textual coherence. Undershaft and Cusins have already been revealed in their Dionysian patterns, but now Cusins points to a similar pattern in Barbara. The context, however, failed to draw the sort of acting that was required for Shaw's final scene to reach the apogée of dramatic radiance.

For one thing, the pacing of the Cusins-Undershaft exchange was a little slow, especially as Douglas Rain's speech about the Undershaft line of descent sounded like a pontifical lecture. The text underscores the shock in Cusins' revelation of his true identity as a foundling - which identity qualifies him to be Undershaft's heir. The shock has a co-ordinate tremor: as Barbara recognizes, Cusins is selling his own soul for the sake of wealth and material power. Cusins is represented as "a shark of the first order" by Undershaft, and, so, is perfectly in key with the sinister Machiavellian irony of being a champion of everything that his beloved has fought against. The interplay among the characters is supposed to have a super-human drive all its own:

UNDERSHAFT. From the moment when you become Andrew Undershaft, you will never do as you please again. Dont come here lusting for power, young man.

CUSINS. If power were my aim I should not come here for it. You have no power.

UNDERSHAFT. None of my own, certainly.

CUSINS. I have more power than you, more will. You do not drive this place: it drives you. And what drives the place?

UNDERSHAFT (enigmatically) A will of which I am a part.

Undershaft sees no darkness, no dreadfulness in Perivale St. Andrews - none of the "poverty, misery, cold and hunger" that he has seen in the Salvation shelter. Indeed, he sees himself as a saviour who has rescued his Christian daughter from the seven deadly sins of "Food, clothing, firing, rent, taxes, respectability and children" - the "seven millstones" around man's neck. He claims to have turned his daughter into Major Barbara and saved her from "the crime of poverty." This didactic section does not reduce the sense of a strange possession in the Dionysian characters. Perhaps in Undershaft's case, it is the possession born of his paradoxical moral passion to achieve good by evil means, but it is a powerful driven passion all the same. Unfortunately, Douglas Rain's composure as an actor worked against the larger notes in the role. His easy-going surface and precise diction evoked a rather careful persuader, a crafty debater, much more than an extraordinarily diabolonian prophet. The role is of the same order as that of the Devil in *Man and Superman* or of Shotover in *Heartbreak House*, but with a different surface and range. Undershaft is no mystic, but he is saturated with the kind of energy propounded by a Nietzsche or Blake. Rain, however, was incapable of investing the part with this type of blazing energy. He was paradoxical without being fuliginous, witty without being lambent.

Had Martha Burns' Barbara possessed the full qualities of her role, this deficiency would not have registered as strongly as it did in the final sequences. However, Burns failed with the character's hypnotic ecstasy, which simply magnified the lack of conviction in Shaw's ending. The final scene has its languors, and, as Desmond MacCarthy observed, it is "weak on the stage; indeed the defect of the play is that Barbara's conversion is much less impressive than the loss of her old religion." (MacCarthy 49) One of the reasons is the curious structure and focus. Barbara is frequently displaced in favour of Cusins and Undershaft. She is the most interiorized of the characters, but Shaw does not give her enough text with which to expose her inner workings. Her self-possession curbs the earthquake of her *anagnorisis*, and when the point is reached when Barbara remarks "That is how I feel in this place today. I stood on the rock I thought eternal; and without a word of warning it reeled and crumbled under me," the audience is meant to feel the force of her dizzying crumbling. Shaw builds an image of someone trembling on the brink of catastrophe. Barbara's self-possession is dissolving in the tension of a portentous waiting, but Martha Burns took the passage too quietly, too full of uncomplicated meditativeness. When, near the end, the actress grew more animated - prompted, in part, by Mezon's swinging her around in jubilation on "Oh for my drum!" - the dynamics did not suffice. Burns attempted large gestures - even to the point of stretching out her hands in parody of a crucifixion pose - but these did nothing to achieve power for her transfiguration. At this point, Barbara has rid herself of "the bribe of bread" and "the bribe of heaven." She wants God's work to be done "for its own sake: the work he had to create us to do because it cannot be done except by living men and women." Her diction and rhetoric become more daringly assertive, blending Scriptural echoes with personal vibrations. She becomes, like Saint Joan, a woman of extraordinary resolve, but instead of a martyrdom, she achieves a realistic militancy and childlike eagerness. In actuality, the change is too much for any actress to ring thoroughly:

> Oh, did you think my courage would never come back? did you believe that I was a deserter? that I, who have stood in the streets, and taken my people to my heart, and talked of the holiest and greatest things with them, could ever turn back and chatter foolishly to fashionable people about nothing in a drawing room? Never, never, never, never: Major Barbara will die with the colours. Oh! and I have my dear little Dolly boy still; and he has found me my place and my work. Glory Hallelujah!

This speech is an aria, whether a contemporary director and his actress wish to render it so or not. It has an operatic quality, but its basis in emotional truth is questionable. Has Barbara been telling the truth about her religion up to this act? Is she really disgusted by her father's "religion" of gunpowder and money? Has she also been lying to Cusins, thereby deepening the irony of his own admission of hypocrisy and dissimulation? It is a problem that Shaw himself was unable to resolve. When Rex Harrison and Wendy Hiller asked Shaw for help on the scene for their 1940 film (produced by Gabriel Pascal), he read it over and said, "This is a terrible scene," and walked away. (Leary 184) Earlier, Shaw had muttered to Gilbert Murray (the model for Cusins), "I don't know how to end the thing." (Smith 376) The unalterable fact, then, is that any actress has to find some way of making the character's journey from Christian idealism to moral compromise credible. Perhaps Shaw's major reason for writing the aria was to attempt to cover up the psychological deficiency in the role.

Newton's production attempted a punchy, comic ending, with Barbara kissing Cusins so violently that he fell down the steps and lay prone through her final lines. Burns' sudden giddy emotion was a jubilation in counterpoint to her religious ecstasy. It became childish, as well, in her demand for a house she could share with "Dolly" in the village, and in her beseechment of her mother for advice. When she exited, it was Undershaft who had the final line for Cusins ("Six o'clock tomorrow morning, Euripides"), confirming Undershaft's oversswaying power. Although joy was part of the final picture, Newton's blocking -

with Douglas Rain on the top step - made it clear that the real power of the story was still Undershaft's.

CHAPTER SEVEN

YOU NEVER CAN TELL

In addition to being a comedy about people who suffer and love, celebrate and bemoan their lives, *You Never Can Tell* is an experiment with comedy, that allows passion, reason, and crazy fun to co-exist and lead to a poetic negative capability - an attitude that enables characters to reconcile themselves to a life of unexpected happenings and mysterious ends. This attitude is evoked so strangely, so unpredictably, and with such a startling mixture of grotesque and delicate images, that the play might well appear to some people to be a total fantasy, a kind of fairly free-wheeling exercise of Shaw's comic imagination to illuminate the freedom and arbitrariness of life. That Shaw exploits the familiar conventions of *Commedia dell'Arte*, Shakespeare, Attic comedy, tragedy, and Victorian drawing-room comedy merely adds to the beautiful strangeness, for this is one of his most experimental plays that is part extravagant fable, part allegory, part comic romance, and part farcical metaphor of the freedom of comic art.

Using different keys for several of his characters, Shaw manages to keep the overall tone delicately off-centre and strangely sour-sweet. Margery Morgan has discussed the autobiographical element in the play, but Shaw was not after sublimated or disguised autobiography, and there is no need to rehearse her discussion here. Instead it is far more fruitful to attend to the strange little notes I have already mentioned. The names of several of the characters have associations with romance: Valentine, Gloria, even Dolly (whose pet name adds an element of child's play to the formal "Dorothy"). Embedded in such names are ideas of springtime, the blossoming of love and youth. But the image of Valentine's dentist's chair jars such associations with pure innocence. There is a hint of pain - even though this pain will be anaesthetized. Dolly's burlesque line "'Pluck from the memory a rooted sorrow.' With gas, five shillings extra" achieves several effects: it makes light of Crampton's "twinge of memory" ("I don't forget injuries"), and of the unpleasantness of dental surgery, and it offers a metaphor - via Shakespeare - of the art of this play. Shaw moves in and out of farce, romance, and satire. Valentine, Crampton, and Mrs. Clandon introduce varying degrees of melancholy. Valentine's lament, "My conscience has been my ruin," is not made lugubriously, but its very sprightliness is jarringly comic and, so, an evident disguise for some dissatisfaction. Mrs. Clandon, who has perversely cut off her children from England and their father, carries some vague pain in her soul - perhaps as a consequence of an unhappy marriage. And Crampton, the comic Lear of the piece, is embittered by some unspecified emotional injury. So, pain is the psychological verity under the comedy, and the light-heartedness of much of the dialogue, the harlequinade of the final scene, and the concluding dance simply underscore Shaw's bittersweet undertones.

The play is surrealistic in its heightenings of reality, its flexible modulations of mood and rhythm, and its free mixture of symbolic associations. Mrs. Clandon, the errant wife, is a former member of The Dialectical Society and, as critics claim, a close spiritual relative of Ibsen's Nora. She and her old friend M'Comas (whose name comically suggests a coma) are left behind by the *avant-garde* and are in an intellectual limbo. Gloria is rational to the point of inhumanity - almost like Vivie Warren - but she is changed by love. Moods change. Mrs. Clandon and Crampton engage in a passionate duel of the sexes. Gloria's conflicts of mind and heart make for a particularly interesting love-scene with Valentine. The gay twins are Harlequin and Columbine in the final act. And the mysteriously wry comic Waiter (nicknamed "William" after Shakespeare) "supplies the mood and tone within which the whole range of emotion, from unshadowed gaiety to disillusionment and despair, can be safely contained." (Morgan 92) Bohun appears in a grotesque mask to usher the characters into the final dance, but his appearance is rather chilling and counterpoints William's humane and patient humour. The rich mixture of moods and modes shows that the play is festive and shows no anxiety about the odds against its craft. Shaw was able to be much freer in his writing than he might have been had he fretted over pleasing only a single segment of his audience.

The 1988 production established an airy, light-hearted tone, beginning with Cameron Porteous' skeleton set - free-standing, spindly white pillars, arches, and lattice work set against a wide blue sky. The minimalism - except for the imposing dentist chair in Act I and the artificial white gulls that sat like silent voyeurs atop the pillars - was dictated by the exigencies of touring the play. Porteous had to invent a set that could fit into a truck, would store in a space not more than eight feet wide, fourteen feet high, and twenty-five feet long, and that would not require a flying system. His pre-production meetings with Newton generated an unequivocal image - that of a dentist's chair, though the two men batted around images of beaches and holiday resorts of the type found on tourist postcards. Shaw's text calls for a dentist's operating room in a furnished lodging in a sea-front terrace in Devon, followed by the terrace of the Marine Hotel, and the Clandons' expensive hotel sitting-room. Porteous devised an environment that had a feeling of the sea, air, clouds, and sky. He went for atmosphere rather than dense detail, so that he could preserve the festive mood. For the pillars and terrace colonnade he copied the architecture of old English seaside hotels likely to be found in Torquay or Devon. He originally designed a frieze of a half-dozen naked actors plastered over to suggest a Parthenon relief. This idea was inspired by a San Francisco performance artist who had sprayed himself with concrete grey paint, strapped himself to a chair on a rooftop, where he sat and talked all day in the third person as if he were a living frieze. Newton admired this surrealist idea, but foresaw a problem for his actors who would be required to perform under a group of naked men. The seagulls were an acceptable, diversionary delight - not at all distracting once the audience had taken notice of them, for they sat immobile, except for a brief mechanical flapping of wings at the end of the play. In keeping with the airiness of mood, Porteous had carpets and upholstery in fabrics with painted cloud shapes. The dominant blue sky made for a feeling of openness, and the serene colours prevented any sense of stuffiness that often mars Shavian stage décor.

The lightness of design was matched by a lightness of background music. Christopher Donison composed a score that ranged from a wind and brass pier band to a lush ballroom orchestra, but, in general, the score was dominated by waltzes (including an eight-bar tune of Shaw's own devising, a jazz waltz for the signature theme, a quasi-Chopin waltz for piano and orchestra, and a quasi-Strauss waltz). The opening fanfare evoked Elgar, but ended on a note and held pitch that merged with the sound of the dentist drill. The surrealistic device cleverly married the idea of frivolity to that of pain, drawing subtle attention to the fact that the play has real pain beneath its light-heartedness.

The first act is Shaw's exposition, in which we are given suggestions of some gravity beneath the surface frivolity and careless humour of the gay twins (who speak charmingly timed duets of automatic interweavings), Mrs. Clandon's cool, self-possessed wit, Valentine's boyish self-confidence, and Gloria's fastidious pride. Newton's direction successfully emphasized the *leitmotif* of pain. This was not going to be a romp without heart or mind. This was going to be a farce with seeds of tragedy.

The idea of pain is represented by the dentist's chair. As Dolly says to Valentine: "it's your business not to hurt people." But this is mere physical pain that can be numbed by drugs or by sheer willpower, as Crampton attempts to do by the end of the act, until Valentine overpowers him by the mouthpiece for an anaesthetic. Although the glint of Valentine's forceps and the ineffective struggle of Crampton are the last things an audience sees in Act I, it is not physical pain that underscores the ineffable, inchoate sadness. In Newton's production, the glittering comedy of manners - reminiscent of Oscar Wilde - was not allowed to overpower the hints of emotional pain. There was something vaguely unsettling about the sprightly, mechanically witty virtuosity of the twins. In their automatic duets, Helen Taylor and Steven Sutcliffe made merry with dithyrambic, confident exclamations - all bright and clever - yet also indicating something awkwardly upsetting, because we wondered whether this sort of playfulness was not simply a facade to conceal an impatience with English manners. They were wont to treat the world as an object of absurdity, but by their concerted gaiety and automatism, they, too, became absurd. Their spontaneous burlesquing of Gloria ("Learning's daughter! Madeira's pride! Beauty's paragon!") and their mother ("No household is complete without her works. We came to England to get away from them") sometimes revealed a cold insensitivity to others' feelings, but, after all, they are the product of an unhappy marriage.

You Never Can Tell demonstrates some of the nefarious effects of a failed marriage and the idiosyncratic education of children. Mrs. Clandon, a brilliant feminist, is vindictive towards her estranged husband. She deliberately refuses to divulge his identity to her children, and quietly but forcefully reminds Gloria of Crampton's use of corporal punishment. She also declares: "Your father is nothing to you, nor to me." For his own part, Crampton carries his own bitter feelings: "I don't forget injuries: and I don't want to forget them." A toothache is only minor pain to him, and what afflicts him is memory of his marriage.

In a way, Frances Hyland's brittle composure and Sandy Webster's flummoxed outrage were in keeping with Newton's subtle tone, for the actors were quite content to leave us wondering about the subtext to this marital warfare. Besides, Shaw's text is gradualist in its careful deepening of dark notes - rather like Shakespeare's way of mixing comedy and heaviness in *Twelfth Night* and *Much Ado About Nothing*.

In Act II Shaw increases the pitch and poignancy of the subject of mismatched partners and mismatched parents and children, without ever diminishing the comic insouciance. The principal incidents in this section are the Clandon dinner, at which Crampton takes umbrage over his treatment by his own children, and the extraordinary love scene between Gloria and Valentine, which quakes with the most intimate passions. However, once again there are elements of pain in this act, but the old, wise servant, William, is employed as a very patient, sympathetic chorus and intermediary who restores humane feeling at moments when others are quite put out of countenance.

Once more Shaw begins on notes of incongruity - this time with the appearance of M'Comas (Mrs. Clandon's former suitor and now her family solicitor). Robert Benson's respectability on the sunny terrace set off associations with mad dogs and Englishmen, as his massive bulk was stuffed into a London frock-coat, with gloves, silk hat, and umbrella to complete the eccentric picture. But this Englishman was really more the old guard left behind the times in his Philosophic Radicalism than the eccentric colonial of Kipling's or Coward's vintage. M'Comas has been enlisted by Mrs. Clandon to break the identity of their father to the children, but when the children entered (the girls with dainty parasols), they immediately refused to accept M'Comas' information or authority. They audaciously insisted on their right to select their own father, with Philip's asking William to be their father.

It is here that William's true role emerges. He is not simply the conventional comic butler of English farce or satire. He is not merely the wise chorus dispensing homespun wisdom for his employers and betters, while remaining aloof from the main action. Although he is more often than not on the periphery of the action -ushering in two other waiters, supervising the dinner party, and serving drinks - he weaves in and out of the conversation, helps to soothe wounded feelings, and points the play in a direction of calm acquiescence to the vagaries of fortune. As played to silken, elegant perfection by Douglas Rain, William was a cheerful restorer of benign sentiment. His exquisitely slow delivery, with ever a trace of gentle melody, and his perfect social tact and manners made his sagacity all the more appealing. In a gathering storm of conflicting wills and attitudes, he remained the calm centre, able to indicate the magic of the place and the magic of the play. Where Crampton was the family Lear by way of Dickens, William was unruffled Old Father William of nursery rhyme fame, "the most thoughtful of men" in Philip's words. The father of a son who was now an important barrister, William offered an existential philosophy to soothe souls in turmoil: "Well, sir, you never can tell. Thats a principle in life with me, sir, if youll excuse my having such a thing, sir....Yes, sir, you never can tell. There was my son, sir! who ever thought that he would rise to wear a silk gown, sir? And yet, today, sir, nothing less than fifty guineas. What a lesson, sir!'' It was in William's nature to point to the hotel as ''a refuge from home life,'' and to the unfolding present as a thing of ever unexpected wonder and surprise, but as yet none of the others was able to subscribe to his wisdom. Mrs. Clandon sought to remove herself from the ultimate confrontation between her children and their true father. Crampton demanded his due of ''Duty, affection, respect, obedience'' as the father, and Gloria strove to be her mother's daughter in her stubbornly principled pride and anti-sentimentality (''I obey nothing but my sense of what is right. I respect nothing that is not noble. That is my duty. As to affection, it is not within my control. I am not sure that I quite know what affection means''). It was soon her time to find out the extent of her self-delusion.

But the real revelation of this section was in the comedy of resisted sentiment between Gloria and Valentine, which glowed with deep, disturbing passion. Mary Haney's Gloria effected a starchily polite contempt for pretty speeches and for marriage proposals, but her manner was a mask to hide the vulnerable creature she really was in terms of her innermost feelings. On the surface, she was vehement in her detestation of weakness and sentiment, and this made her seem a strong attraction to Andrew Gillies' Valentine, who was plainly dazzled by her inspiring declaration. But in describing the miracle of his rejuvenation, Gillies' Valentine exuded a certain dread of what might happen next - a note immediately shared by Haney's Gloria, who turned uneasy with the same presentiment. She proposed a scientific explanation for this mysterious effect, but was quickly offset by Valentine's intuitive understanding of nature's powers. This was a moment of delicious Shavian satire:

> GLORIA. I wonder what is the scientific explanation of those fancies that cross us occasionally!
> VALENTINE. Ah, I wonder? It's a curiously helpless sensation: isnt it?
> GLORIA. [*rebelling against the word*] Helpless?
> VALENTINE. Yes, helpless. As if Nature, after letting us belong to ourselves and do what we judged right and reasonable for all these years, were suddenly lifting her great hand to take us - her two little children - by the scruffs of our little necks, and use us, in spite of ourselves, for her own purposes, in her own way.

Such a moment crystallized Shaw's surreal feeling, and the acting of Haney and Gillies conveyed the magic of this enchantment. The harder Haney's Gloria tried to be objective and rational about her feeling, the more vulnerable she became to a sexual attraction to Valentine. And the more emphatically sceptical Gillies' Valentine grew about the evidence of his own eyes, heart, instincts, and imagination, the stronger was his compulsion to submit to the "illusion" of romance. The spectacle of the two attempting to understand their own racing heartbeats was extraordinary proof of Shaw's ability to reveal the ecstasy of love in a middle range - not the grand ecstasy of opera or classical tragedy, nor the scale of Victorian melodrama, but a very credible agitation of mind and soul reminiscent of the passion of Ann Whitefield and Jack Tanner in *Man and Superman*. The extent of the ecstasy could be gauged from Valentine's rhetoric: "Whats this place? it's not heaven: it's the Marine Hotel. Whats the time? it's not eternity: it's about half past one in the afternoon. What am I? a dentist: a five shilling dentist!" The juxtaposition of the sublime and the ridiculous made for a poignant comedy, and pain rippled through the duet. Valentine was in agony: "Your voice is tearing my heart to pieces. Let me alone, Gloria. You go down into the very depths of me, troubling and stirring me. I cant struggle with it....It's all over: we're in love with one another." Their image of a violent tearing asunder and of a descent into some psychological maelstrom was not meant to be comic in itself, but was made so only because of the lovers' attempt to resist what was becoming plainly inevitable. Now Valentine - associated with pain by his surgical instruments - was the one to suffer, just as Crampton had at the dinner, and as Mrs. Clandon had in her marriage. But the curtain went to Gloria who, in reproaching her mother ("Why didn't you educate me properly?"), showed a true helplessness in the face of romantic love.

Act III would organically elaborate on Gloria's perplexities of shame and ardour. The biscuit-coloured twins made fun of their sister (and of their mother, in the bargain), and another sharp strain in this section was the disclosure of Mrs. Clandon's fear of the open heart. In effect, Act III could have been divided into two major parts: the impassioned duet between Gloria and Valentine, ever deepening and disturbing, though as yet unresolved; and the equally impassioned contest between Mrs. Clandon and Crampton over custody of the children. In the first case, Shaw manifests an overt drama of will and heart; in the second, he allows subtext to infuse the action with potency.

Mrs. Clandon exerts a large influence on both parts. In attempting to protect Gloria from Valentine's advances, she shows her own ignorance about matters of love: "I am going to speak of a subject of which I know very little: perhaps nothing. I mean love." But what charges her vehement defensiveness of Gloria is not mere distrust of Valentine, but a general cynicism about men, prompted by her own marital disappointment. No wonder, then, that love and romance have been displaced by humanitarian causes and ideals: "Let me tell you, Mr. Valentine, that a life devoted to the Cause of Humanity has enthusiasms and passions to offer which far transcend the selfish personal infatuations and sentimentalities of romance. Those are not your enthusiasms and passions, I take it?" She sounds very much like a socialist philosopher. Yet we must wonder whether Shaw is being subtly satirical at her expense. Unfortunately, in her reading of this passage, Frances Hyland scanted on the melancholy or bittersweet sadness of the character in favour of a severely intelligent, brisk candour.

Hyland's tone sharpened the debate between Mrs. Clandon and Valentine on the battle of the sexes, in which Valentine draws an analogy with artillery: "You build a ship proof against the best gun known: somebody makes a better gun and sinks your ship. You build a heavier ship, proof against that gun: somebody makes a heavier gun and sinks you again. And so on. Well, the duel of sex is just like that." In this crisp exchange between the clever young "five shilling" dentist and the old-fashioned mother, romance and love are wittily demythicized, only to eventually heighten Valentine's astonishment at the extent and depth of his own involvement in a sex duel with Gloria. The more Mrs. Clandon views Valentine as a dangerous seducer, and the more Gloria pretends to be subjugated by the laws of Creative Evolution, the funnier becomes the lovers' vulnerability to soul-shaking passions.

Mrs. Clandon has subverted her own heart, but she gives only hints or incomplete disclosures of what went wrong in her marriage: "I never discovered his feelings. I discovered his temper, and his - [she shivers] the rest of his common humanity." And as Crampton is unable to articulate the source of his own wounded feelings, it is left to M'Comas to serve as chorus in this regard. Strangely enough, it is Crampton who earns pity - perhaps because Mrs. Clandon is so unforgiving and so unaware of her own influence on Gloria, who has evidently learned form her mother to mistrust her own heart.

Act III moves, through the help of a *deus ex machina*, to a point of mediation in the custody dispute, but the pacific mood of the closing is achieved by the regatta fancy dress ball. The mood is precipitated by William, who announces, "the band and the arranging of the fairy lights and one thing or another." The romantic glow of Robert Thomson's lighting, and the economy of Cameron Porteous' décor (mainly Chinese lanterns) and Christopher Newton's direction suffused the final movement of Act III with a surreal radiance. Valentine's confession about his infatuation with Gloria, and her professed disapproval had mellow grace notes. Gillies' Valentine grew poetic in his newfound astonishment: "Love cant give any man new gifts. It can only heighten the gifts he was born with.... The whole world is like a feather dancing in the light now; and Gloria is the sun.'' Gillies had become a Romeo, and Mary Haney a miscalculating Juliet who, embarrassed by his passion, assumed a hauteur that did nothing to stop his gay exit.

The final act puts Shaw's plot machinery in full gear. Both Crampton and Gloria are found to be helpless in the face of impulse and circumstance, but both are shown to possess ''a melancholy sense of humour, though humour is not their strong point.'' Both gain an audience's pathos for their respective humiliations. Gloria, who had been ''high and mighty,'' has come down considerably, and Crampton, so dogmatic about paternal rights and filial duties, now surrenders his righteous indignation - except in the matter of his marriage. The ''magical'' appearance of Bohun (''dropped down on us out of the clouds'') is to lead to a solution of the Clandon domestic dispute, but even so intellectually sharp and imposing a legal authority cannot clarify or control the workings of romantic love. Bohun is important for three main reasons: he seems to end the custody battle; he exemplifies the validity of his father's belief in existential unpredictability; and he is an ironic counter to the romantic duel between Gloria and Valentine, in that his ruthlessly efficient legal mind and vocal authority (described by Shaw as an annihilating thunderbolt) are inadequate forces to control the mysterious workings of the human heart. Bohun's speciality is ''being right when other people are wrong,'' and while he can be ''a boon and a blessing'' - in Dolly's pun on his name - to his father and clients, he is, finally, at the mercy of unpredictable romance. Even his fairly sinister or grotesque costume for the ball cannot preserve him from being caught up in the ''magic'' of the harlequinade, and in the agitated romance of Gloria and Valentine, he can play no active part, being swept up himself in the mirth and frivolity of the regatta ball.

Newton's production was so exquisitely wrought as to bring home to an audience Shaw's extraordinary balancing of levity and gravity, intellectual argument and emotional tremors. With the appearance of the twins in Harlequin and Columbine costumes (and set to waltz music in the background), it was clear that the twins ''have been Harlequin and Columbine all the time, and their contemporary dress - not this - was the disguise.'' (Morgan 90-91) It is Bohun who says of Dolly: ''You'd want this young lady here to give up dressing like a stage columbine in the evening and like a fashionable columbine in the morning.'' Philip's bat was waved like a magic wand, and before darting away, he quoted Shakespeare's Ariel.

But these clever visual and verbal transformations were only tonal modifications for the most telling comedy of enlightenment to come shortly. Valentine and Gloria were left to the reciprocal symmetry of their wounded feelings: they had made much the same speeches to former "lovers" as they had to each other, and both were now to throw off the false manners of their romantic slavery in order to acquire the genuine manners of their romantic freedom. Both finally recognized that they had been Nature's jest in the womb of time - but not before one more quake or tremor. Both were in real emotional pain: Valentine felt that Gloria had never truly cared for him; Gloria's pride had prevented her from revealing her true feelings. Valentine (in Gillies' charmingly athletic, springy deportment) stepped up the pressure and pace, attempting to attain some control, struggling to win not only the Gloria of his imagination, but the flesh-and-blood Gloria as well. Finally, Gloria yielded. Her pride thawed, and in the production Mary Haney showed clearly (by a deft alteration in body language or intonation) Gloria's risky submission to her own real feelings. This little scene had a poignant reality - rather like the final shared intimacy between Ann and Jack in *Man and Superman* - for the two lovers now faced up to each other in delicious nervousness. Valentine recognized the perfect madness: "If we go out to dance together I shall have to borrow five shillings from her for a ticket Gloria: dont be rash: youre throwing yourself away....I'm frightened, I'm positively frightened; and thats the plain truth." Was any other Shavian lover ever so vulnerably, so achingly honest? This was Shaw's surrealism as a moment of exquisitely poignant expectancy - a quivering hope for paradise, a dream of mediating between limitation and the marvellous. Valentine was taking to heart William's precept not to let a matter of five shillings stand between him and happiness. And it was William who had the last word, as he contemplated the "defeated Duellist of Sex with ineffable benignity":

> Cheer up, sir, cheer up. Every man is frightened of marriage when it comes to the point; but it often turns out very comfortable, very enjoyable and happy indeed, sir - from time to time. *I* never was master in my own house, sir: my wife was like your young lady: she was of a commanding and masterful disposition, which my son has inherited. But if I had my life to live twice over, I'd do it again: I'd do it again, I assure you. You never can tell, sir: you never can tell.

Gone, then, in the consolations of romance and William's philosophy were the teasing pain of a false life. But other pain was not absent. Crampton still earned pathos; Mrs. Clandon, a modicum of sympathy for a hard-earned autonomy; and their children, understanding for the negative side of the puritanism they had battled. Gone, too, was Valentine's social indignity as a mere five shilling dentist, and Bohun's cold, authoritarian intellect. The final image was not the dentist's chair, but the flapping gulls atop the spindly pillars. Love and wisdom had awakened the birds from indifference. They seemed to applaud the audience in recognition of some shared revelations about human beings at the mercy of the ineffable freedom of life. And a waltz, that had played all through William's final speech, gaining momentum and orchestration, now erupted into something grand for the curtain.

Scene from <u>Caesar and Cleopatra</u> (1983), with <u>(L-R. rear)</u> Susan Stackhouse as Charmian and Diane Douglass as Ftatateeta. <u>(Photo: David Cooper. Courtesy of the photographer).</u>

Scene from <u>Caesar and Cleopatra</u> (1983), with (<u>L-R</u>) Herb Foster as Brittanus, Keith Knight as Courtier, John Gilbert as Major Domo, Douglas Rain as Caesar, Leonard Chow as Courtier, and Marti Maraden as Cleopatra. (<u>Photo: David Cooper. Courtesy of the photographer</u>).

Scene from <u>Caesar and Cleopatra</u> (1983). (<u>Photo: David Cooper. Courtesy of the photographer</u>).

Carole Shelley as Lina Szczepanowska in <u>Misalliance</u> (1980). <u>(Photo: David Cooper. Courtesy of the University of Guelph Library Archival Collections).</u>

Nora McLellan as <u>Saint Joan</u> (1981), <u>(Photo: David Cooper. Courtesy of the University of Guelph Library Archival Collections.</u>

*Jack Medley as Archbishop of Rheims and Richard Farrell
as Duc de la Tremouille in Saint Joan (1981). (Photo: David Cooper.
Courtesy of the University of Guelph Library Archival Collections).*

*The Dauphin's Cart from Saint Joan (1981). (Photo: David
Cooper. Courtesy of the photographer).*

Scene from <u>Saint Joan</u> (1981), with (L-R) Duncan McIntosh as Page to Dunois and Peter Dvorsky as Dunois. (Photo: David Cooper. Courtesy of the photographer).

The tent scene from <u>Saint Joan</u> (1981), with (L-R) Barry MacGregor as Stogumber, Robert Benson as Warwick, and David Hemblen as Cauchon, (Photo: David Cooper. Courtesy of the photographer).

Scene from <u>Saint Joan</u> (1981), with <u>(L-R, front)</u> Nora McLellan as Saint Joan, Jack Medley as Archbishop, and Heath Lamberts as the Dauphin. <u>(Photo: David Cooper. Courtesy of the photographer)</u>. ▸

Scene from <u>Saint Joan</u> (1981), with <u>(L-R, front)</u> Tom McCamus as Brother Martin, Nora McLellan as Saint Joan, and David Hemblen as Cauchon. <u>(Photo: David Cooper. Courtesy of the photographer)</u>.

Scene from <u>Heartbreak House</u> (1985), with <u>(L-R)</u> Marti Maraden as Ellie Dunn, Jim Jones and Ric Sarabia as Gardener's Boys. <u>(Photo: David Cooper. Courtesy of the photographer)</u>.

Scene from <u>Heartbreak House</u> (1985), with <u>(L-R)</u> Marti Maraden as Ellie and Goldie Semple as Hesione. <u>(Photo: David Cooper. Courtesy of the photographer)</u>.

Scene from <u>Heartbreak House</u> (1985), with <u>(L-R)</u> Goldie Semple as Hesione, Robert Benson as Boss Mangan, and Allan Gray as Mazzini Dunn. <u>(Photo: David Cooper. Courtesy of the photographer)</u>.

Scene from <u>Heartbreak House</u> (1985), with <u>(L-R)</u> Douglas Rain as Shotover, Allan Gray as Mazzini Dunn; Marti Maraden as Ellie, Fiona Reid as Ariadne, Peter Krantz as Randall Utterword, and Norman Browning as Hector Hushabye. <u>(Photo: David Cooper. Courtesy of the photographer)</u>.

Scene from <u>Heartbreak House</u> (1985), with <u>(L-R)</u> Allan Gray as Mazzini Dunn, Marti Maraden as Ellie, Fiona Reid as Ariadne, Andrew Gillies as Burglar, Norman Browning as Hector, and Peter Krantz as Randall. <u>(front)</u> Goldie Semple as Hesione. <u>(Photo: David Cooper. Courtesy of the photographer)</u>.

Scene from <u>Heartbreak House</u> (1985), with Douglas Rain as Shotover and Marti Maraden as Ellie. <u>(Photo: David Cooper. Courtesy of the University of Guelph Library Archival Collections)</u>.

Scene from <u>Heartbreak House</u> (1985), with <u>(L-R)</u> Jennifer Phipps as Nurse Guinness, Fiona Reid as Ariadne, Peter Krantz as Randall, Allan Gray as Mazzini, Marti Maraden as Ellie, Norman Browning as Hector, and Douglas Rain as Shotover. <u>(Photo: David Cooper. Courtesy of the University of Guelph Library Archival Collections).</u>

Scene from <u>Major Barbara</u> (1987), with Steven Sutcliffe as Stephen Undershaft and Frances Hyland as Lady Undershaft. <u>(Photo: David Cooper. Courtesy of the photographer).</u>

Douglas Rain as Andrew Undershaft in <u>Major Barbara</u> (1987). <u>(Photo: David Cooper. Courtesy of the photographer)</u>.

Scene from <u>Misalliance</u> (1990), with (<u>L-R</u>) Barry MacGregor as Tarleton, Jennifer Phipps as Mrs Tarleton, Sharry Flett as Lina Szczepanowska, Mark Burgess as Johnny Tarleton, and Helen Tay as Hypatia. <u>(Photo: David Coope Courtesy of the University of Gu Library Archival Collections)</u>.

Scene from Major Barbara *(1987), with Martha Burns as Barbara and Steven Sutcliffe as Stephen Undershaft. (Photo: David Cooper. Courtesy of the Shaw Festival.)*

Scene from Major Barbara *(1987), with (L-R) Ted Dykstra as Snobby Price, Helen Taylor as Jenny Hill, Martha Burns as Barbara, and Jon Bryden as Bill Walker. (Photo: David Cooper. Courtesy of the photographer).*

Scene from <u>Major Barbara</u> (1987), with <u>(L-R, rear)</u> Helen Taylor as Jenny Hill, Grant Carmichael as Salvation Army Worker, Jennifer Phipps as Mrs. Baines, and Jon Bryden as Bill Walker. <u>(L-R, front)</u> Martha Burns as Barbara and Jim Mezon as Cusins. <u>(Photo: David Cooper. Courtesy of the photographer).</u>

Scene from <u>Major Barbara</u> (1987), with Martha Burns as Barbara and Douglas Rain as Undershaft. <u>(Photo: David Cooper. Courtesy of the photographer).</u>

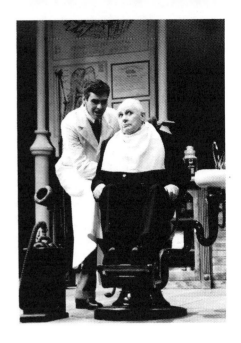

*Martha Burns in <u>Major Barbara</u> (1987).
Photo: David Cooper. Courtesy of the
photographer).*

*Scene from <u>You Never Can Tell</u> (1988),
with (<u>L-R</u>) Andrew Gillies as Valentine
and Sandy Webster as Crampton. (<u>Photo:
David Cooper. Courtesy of the photo-
grapher</u>.*

*Scene from <u>Misalliance</u> (1990), with Simon Bradbury as Gunner (Julius Baker) and
Barry MacGregor as Tarleton. <u>(Photo: David Cooper. Courtesy of the Shaw Festival)</u>.*

Scene from <u>You Never Can Tell</u> (1988), with <u>(L-R)</u> Douglas Rain as The Waiter and Robert Benson as M'Comas. <u>(Photo: David Cooper. Courtesy of the photographer).</u>

Scene from <u>You Never Can Tell</u> (1988), with Andrew Gillies as Valentine and Mary Haney as Gloria. <u>(Photo: David Cooper. Courtesy of the photographer)</u>.

Scene from <u>Misalliance</u> (1980), with <u>(L-R)</u> Carole Shelley as Lina Szczepanowska, Sandy Webster as Tarleton, Marion Gilsenan as Mrs. Tarleton, Deborah Kipp as Hypatia, Geraint Wyn Davies as Joey Percival, James Rankin as Bentley, and David Dodimead as Lord Summerhays. <u>(Photo: David Cooper. Courtesy of the University of Guelph Library Archival Collections)</u>.

Scene from <u>You Never Can Tell</u> (1988), with <u>(L-R)</u> Barbara Gordon as Mrs. Clandon, Helen Taylor as Dolly, and Steven Sutcliffe as Phillip. <u>(Photo: David Cooper. Courtesy of the photographer)</u>.

Scene from <u>You Never Can Tell</u> (1988). <u>(Photo: David Cooper. Courtesy of the photographer).</u>

Scene from <u>Man and Superman</u> (1989), with Kate Trotter as Ann Whitefield and Michael Ball as John Tanner. <u>(Photo: David Cooper. Courtesy of the Shaw Festival and Scott McKowen).</u>

Scene from the Calgary production of You Never Can Tell (1988), with (L-R) Frances Hyland as Mrs. Clandon, Douglas Rain as The Waiter, Andrew Gillies as Valentine, Steven Sutcliffe as Philip, Jim Mezon as Bohun, Camille Mitchell as Gloria, Helen Taylor as Dolly, and Robert Benson as M'Comas. (Photo: David Cooper. Courtesy of the photographer).

Scene from Man and Superman (1989). (Photo: David Cooper. Courtesy of the Shaw Festival).

William Hutt as Roebuck Ramsden in <u>Man and Superman</u> (1989). <u>(Photo: David Cooper. Courtesy of the photographer).</u>

Scene from <u>Man and Superman</u> (1989), with Kate Trotter as Ann Whitefield and Michael Ball as John Tanner. <u>(Photo: David Cooper. Courtesy of the Shaw Festival and Scott McKowen).</u>

Scene from <u>Man and Superman</u> (1989), with Kate Trotter as Ann Whitefield and Michael Ball as John Tanner. <u>(Photo: David Cooper. Courtesy of the photographer).</u>

Barry MacGregor as The Devil in <u>Man and Superman</u> (1989). (<u>Photo: David Cooper.</u>
<u>Courtesy of the Shaw Festival and Scott McKowen</u>).

Costume and Set Drawing by Eduard Kochergin for <u>Man and Superman</u> (1989)
<u>(Photo: David Cooper. Courtesy of the Shaw Festival and Scott McKowen</u>).

Scene from <u>Man and Superman</u> (1989), with <u>(L-R)</u> William Vickers as Henry Straker and Michael Ball as John Tanner. <u>(Photo: David Cooper. Courtesy of the Shaw Festival and Scott McKowen).</u>

Scene from <u>Man and Superman</u> (1989), with <u>(L-R, front)</u> Tom Wood as Duval and William Vickers as Henry Straker. <u>(Photo: David Cooper. Courtesy of the Shaw Festival and Scott McKowen).</u>

Scene from <u>Man and Superman</u> (1989), with <u>(rear)</u> Peter Krantz as Octavius and <u>(front)</u> William Hutt as Roebuck Ramsden. <u>(Photo: David Cooper. Courtesy of the Shaw Festival)</u>.

Scene from <u>Man and Superman</u> (1989), with <u>(L-R)</u> Michael Ball as John Tanner and Kate Trotter as Ann Whitefield. <u>(Photo: David Cooper. Courtesy of the photographer)</u>.

*Scene from <u>Man and Superman</u> (1989), with <u>(L-R, rear)</u> Marion Gilsenan
as Miss Ramsden, Peter Krantz as Octavius, Barry MacGregor as
Mendoza, Patric Masurkevitch as Hector Malone, William Hutt as
Roebuck Ramsden, Al Kozlik as Mr. Malone; <u>(L-R, front)</u> Julie Stewart
as Violet Robinson, Kate Trotter as Ann Whitefield, and Michael Ball
as John Tanner. <u>(Photo: David Cooper. Courtesy of the photographer)</u>.*

*Scene from <u>Misalliance</u> (1990), with <u>(L-R)</u> Richard Farrell as Lord Summerhays, Barry
MacGregor as Tarleton, Peter Krantz as Joey Percival, and Helen Taylor as Hypatia.
<u>(Photo: David Cooper. Courtesy of the Shaw Festival)</u>.*

Scene from <u>Misalliance</u> (1990), with Peter Krantz as Joey Percival and Helen Taylor as Hypatia. <u>(Photo: David Cooper. Courtesy of the University of Guelph Library Archival Collections.</u>

CHAPTER EIGHT

MAN AND SUPERMAN

Man and Superman was composed at the suggestion of Shaw's friend and fellow critic, Arthur Bingham Walkley, that Shaw address the problem of sexual attraction. In giving his friend a Don Juan play, Shaw was not so much adapting Molina or Mozart to the English stage as creating his own comic "opera" in which man and woman contend with the Life Force. It is reported that in a tense moment during rehearsals for the first production in 1905, Granville Barker, who played Tanner, shouted at the director, Shaw: "It's an opera you've written, not a play." "You're beginning to understand," Shaw replied from the darkened auditorium.

The sheer size and ambition of the play can be daunting to an audience. In a house programme for the 1989 Shaw Festival production, Dan Laurence wrote: "From the first, Shaw conceived of the work in epic proportions, more suitable to an opera house than a West End theatre, with its visionary third-act sequence thought out to be a drama of the thinking man rather than just another conventional examination of the lusting man - a fourth Play for Puritans, in fact - Shaw's play about sex, initially a comedy of manners, unexpectedly metamorphoses into an ultra-religious drama, a comedy of purpose, with conflict (especially in the Hell dream) elevated from a physical to a mental plane."

But the magnitude of the rhetorical score, the calculated sprawl of locales, and the sophisticated orchestration of voices and passions do not obscure the fact that this play is a love chase, in which Jack Tanner, the idle social and philosophical revolutionist, is the quarry of Ann Whitefield, his appointed ward. Sex and love, rather than Nietzschean philosophy, are the potent undercurrent. The whole action may be regarded as a quest in which all the major characters discover something fundamental about life and themselves, so that even the *Don Juan In Hell* sequence becomes an integral part of the overarching action, rather than what Shaw himself (in his Epistle Dedicatory) called ''a totally extraneous act in which my hero, enchanted by the air of the Sierra, has a dream in which his Mozartian ancestor appears and philosophizes at great length in Shavio-Socratic dialogue with the lady, the statue, and the devil.'' (Shaw E xvi)

The epic proportions, the visionary (and decidedly surrealistic) third-act sequence, the comedy, and the ultra-religious drama were all accented in Newton's stunning production, which took the magic of the play very much to heart. Newton saw the play as a magical metamorphosis from comedy of manners to a symbolic ultra-religious comedy of purpose. The superficial correspondences between many of its characters and those in Mozart's *Don Giovanni* were not his preoccupation. His focus was on inversions, for does not Shaw convert the libertine Don Juan into a supreme polemical moralist - and, more than this, a human being who has to be forced or tricked into recognizing his own secret impulses and passions? Of course, John Tanner is no more the Superman (in Nietzsche's sense) than was Don Juan, but he balances the philosophic side of the pamphleteer with the foolish one of a victim preordained to the course of Creative Evolution.

Newton stressed the archetypal quest motif, with special emphases on the super-reality of the adventure. He wrote in the house programme:

This is so much more than the courtship of Ann Whitefield
and Jack Tanner. There is magic here. Theories surprise us
like animals startled by an automobile in the Sierra. It is as
if this giant of an idea is dressed up in conventional
Edwardian middle class clothes; it is as if this giant stretches,
bursts out of this drawing room, and takes us on a miraculous
journey.

Newton and his designer, Eduard Kochergin, award-winning Artist of Merit of the Soviet Union, re-invented Shaw's play in a visual and metaphoric sense. Abandoning his Byzantine preliminaries, Kochergin devised a starkly simple look - largely a bare stage with thin rectangular arches of varying size to frame the actors who played against a background of projections in a vast emptiness. This was, by all conventional standards, a most un-Shavian design, one which prompted a Toronto newspaper critic to sneer to me that it was ''Shaw played between goal posts.''

Shaw subtitled his play "A Comedy and a Philosophy," and made eminently clear in his detailed stage directions for Act I the satiric and philosophic points that were to be made. Ann Whitefield has plotted to have Roebuck Ramsden and Jack Tanner, two men totally opposed to each other, appointed as her co-guardians in her deceased father's will. Her design, of course, is to trap Tanner as her romantic prey while pretending to be his modest ward. The mourning for Mr. Whitefield hardly over, there is more than a hint of sexual sportive play beneath Ann's funereal clothes and appearance. This sport, though cunningly coy, would be shocking to characters who are easily shocked by such things as Violet Robinson's "illicit" pregnancy and by the thunderclap discovery of her secret marriage to young Malone. The action occurs in Ramsden's study; Ramsden is an aging, self-important man of means, unable to see that he is no longer at the forefront of advanced thought. Shaw describes the setting as "handsomely and solidly furnished" and sparklingly clean. Beside a "stately bookcase" there are busts of John Bright and Herbert Spencer, an engraved portrait of Richard Cobden, photographs of Harriet Martineau, Thomas Huxley, and George Eliot, "autotypes of allegories" by G.F. Watts, and "an impression of Dupont's engraving of Delaroche's Beaux Arts hemicycle, representing the great men of all ages."

However valuable and significant such detailed décor might have been to audiences of Shaw's day, it is not really of topical interest today. In fact, it is rather obscure - except with the help of reference books - and the Shaw production ignored it all to establish its own subtle points. When the curtain rose (to the mysterious off-stage sound of a soprano in some invisible room), there was essentially a greyness. There were no words, only open vowel sounds, in Christopher Donison's music for voice and piano, because, as Newton and Donison conceived it, the words had taken off on their own as a prelude to the play's dissociation from purely Edwardian reality. There was an other-worldly feeling, and the fact that the voice was a soprano related to Shaw's idea of the Life Force embodied in a woman or female deity. The piano accompaniment had a link to nineteenth century parlour music, though its harmonic vocabulary was reminiscent to a degree of some of the music of Debussy and Ravel. There were no unnatural key relationships or vocally advanced harmonic concepts, but the overall tenor connected the Edwardian setting to some vague future in which the human spirit would have evolved to a higher plane.

The stage geometry was starkly simple: a set of three rectangular arches, one behind the other in ascending magnitude, and all in a palette of grey and white, with a soft brick hue at the very rear. The only furniture were four high-backed Gothic chairs and a desk to suggest tight and hard moral values. The most vivid counterpoint in colour was the red cover of the *Revolutionist's Handbook* and the red ribbons for the Whitefield will. The only human figure on stage at the opening was Ramsden (William Hutt), first in a grey dressing gown and then in a black frockcoat. The startlingly simple imagery was really Newton's rather than Kochergin's, for the director had perceived the play as moving from cold, sombre greyness to light and heat. Newton had wanted very little colour, except for the striking red that would underline the revolutionary nature of Tanner's character and thought in conflict with the rigid, conventional world of his day. This world was epitomized in the straight-edged geometry of the study, and Ramsden's white hair was not simply meant to show his age, but (as Newton wished) to reveal a man who had apparently gone grey "reading something blood-red and alive." The will changes the lives of Tanner, Ramsden, and Ann, so Newton wanted colour to link it to Hell, sexuality, and chivalry.

The vastness of the stage space at first seemed forbiddingly empty, but the arches and sparse furniture made it three-dimensional. The subtle significance of the arches lay in the generation of the idea of a photographic image, as if the audience were watching an old photograph come to life. Newton recognized that this simple contrivance could become a problem for some actors: "The inexperienced performer would perhaps find difficulty without the carpets and the cushions to hide behind. This set is for the performer who can tell all by raising a finger, who can suggest hidden worlds of emotion by a raised eyebrow or a phrase almost thrown away but ultimately of supreme importance to the development of theme in the play. This space could easily intimidate the beginner because everything points to the actor, and the actor is expected to act."

And the ensemble did act, though, as is becoming his *cachet*, Newton allowed for a very long pause after the curtain before Ramsden's first line. This gave William Hutt the time to establish a grave, though not unfunny mood, as his stage business and demeanour established all those traits of personality that befit Ramsden - "his broad air of importance, his dignified expectation of deference," his "determinate mouth," his comfort, precedence, and power. A parlour maid hurried in to divest him of his silk dressing gown and to assist him into his formal top coat. When Peter Krantz's lachrymose Octavius appeared, Hutt achieved a comic effect from the grave solace he offered: "There! Doesnt that do you good?" Although Krantz's crybaby was sometimes too caricatural and tiresome for someone meant to be a *jeune premier* with "an engaging sincerity and eager modest serviceableness," Hutt's tempered benevolence provided the weight and tone for the opening. With his dominant physique and manner, whether standing by Octavius or seated at his own desk, Hutt gave the opening its shape, playing all the moments for ripe effects. While Krantz lacked conviction in his sentimentality - instead of being eager and embarrassed at mention of Ann's name, he bent over in tearfulness - Hutt compensated by a glorious display of measured technique. He was especially good in his testiness about Tanner's inflammatory book, waxing fulsome in his denunciation, yet getting a large laugh on the title and author's name, and ending with a violent slamming of the book on his desk. But Hutt was not immune to satiric self-exposure. Quite oblivious to his own pompous grandeur, he put Ramsden into a vulnerable position by announcing magisterially, "You know that I am not a bigoted or prejudiced man," revealing in the instant the very opposite of what he espoused. This point would be quickly re-emphasized with Michael Ball's forceful entrance as Tanner, his voice preceding his appearance as he waved the will about before slamming it on the desk and branding Ramsden "an old man with obsolete ideas!"

Although the will is the first shock motif mentioned in the act, there is no formal reading of it. The contents, however, are disclosed, and the main one is the guardianship of Ann, which is to provide the motive power of the action. Rhoda, Ann's younger sister who is mentioned but never seen, is the one who really needs a guardian, but Ann, of an age where she can make use of her own fortune and select her own husband, insists on a guardian as part of her pretence of being weaker than she truly is. Although the sheer volume and prodigious energy of Tanner's speech holds sway in the script, Hutt's Ramsden and Newton's direction did not allow the first act to become a one-man display of bravura rhetorical acting. Perhaps using Shaw's comment that *all* Tanner's moods "are phases of excitement," Ball and his director were able to show just how Tanner's restless fluency and clever humour immerse him in a battle of minds with Ramsden, while blinding him to the real sexual battle to come with Ann.

It is customary for actors to regard the role of Tanner as a huge star-part, full of thrilling arias that are a test of technique. Always one to resist arias in the theatre if they sacrifice sense to beautiful sound, Newton helped Michael Ball put his own stamp on the part, directing him to play it as an intellectually mature but emotionally immature iconoclast, a man of unprepossessing dress but rivetting aphoristic speech, a philosopher without the wisdom of self-insight. Ball played up only three arias in the first act, electing to emphasize, instead, Tanner's candour and sincerity about experience. He seemed to know Ann's manipulative nature without being aware that it was he rather than Octavius who was her real prey. His delivery was exquisitely phrased, while drawing attention more to the thoughts than to the actor's vocal technique, and Ball's intelligence catalyzed his sculpting of the three arias he had decided to highlight. In his first - addressed to Ramsden who had just castigated him for impudence - Ball capitalized on Shaw's subtle grammar and metrical prose which move a single speech of some seventeen lines through three shifts in clausal construction and symmetry. For his second aria he perched on Ramsden's desk, exploiting his trick of exploding unexpectedly on certain words. Here, of course, he was helped by Tanner's vulnerable psyche. Oblivious to the fact that Ann is using the circumstance of her mourning to camouflage her pursuit of Tanner by a playful flirtation with Octavius and insincere deference to her guardians, this Tanner did not show self-insight. The second aria is about "the artist man and the mother woman" and "which shall use up the other," but Tanner did not see that he, rather than Octavius, was the artist man in the process of coming to know himself only because of Ann's power to create him anew.

Much, of course, depends on the actress who plays Ann, for the psychological comedy of Tanner is obtained by the interaction between the two characters. While usually an actress who thrives on emotional acting rather than rhetorical, Kate Trotter was able to modulate quickly from touching appeal to gushing delight and sly wiles. Her technique sometimes showed transparently and there was an occasional strain in her style, but she was effective, all the same. Although Newton deleted Shaw's phrase, "Lady Mephistopheles," the image was intact in the staging, for her costume, manner, and black feather boa all conspired to project the idea of a fatal temptress.

At this point it is necessary to add a word on Kochergin's costuming, which in Act I favoured a sere black against the grey setting. The parlour-maid, Ramsden, Tanner, Ann, Octavius, and Mrs. Whitefield were all in sombre black. Although Ann's costume had an accidental cassocky look, the bizarre movement of the characters was meant to suggest what Newton calls "a strange dance of great black crows flapping around the room." Ann's black was also a predator's grim colour, and a "devilish" camouflage - an austere outwardness for her blood-red inner fires of passion.

The first act moves away from the question of the will and guardianship as soon as the subject of Violet Robinson is brought up. Violet's role in this act is to expose the crippling moral conventionality of Edwardian society, as well as to highlight the themes of hypocrisy and Woman as the Life Force. As Margery Morgan contends, "The *lie* is the dominant motif of the play, reiterated throughout the text, even audible in the Brigand's name, Mendoza; and the action includes a serial demonstration of Ann's mendacity and duplicity." (Morgan 112)

Violet, who is secretly married to and supposedly pregnant by the American Hector Malone, gives the others opportunities to expose their own habits of moral being. Miss Ramsden adopts a censorious attitude to the "fallen" young woman. Ann is affectedly priggish. Octavius and Ramsden are conventionally shocked. Only Tanner has an open mind, and his third aria is about Violet's natural purpose and greatest function - "to increase, multiply, and replenish the earth" - which, despite its crescendo, is really a most conventional, perhaps reactionary view of women. Tanner, however, derives maximum pleasure from ridiculing the others for their hypocritical morality, and Ball's acting made fine fun with the line: "So we are to marry your sister to a damned scoundrel by way of reforming her character?"

The climax of the first act in this production was not Violet's thunderclap disclosure of her marriage - Julie Stewart lacked the *elegant* force that could make the moment startling - but the extended duet between Ann and Jack, once Ann had manoeuvred to have "Granny" Ramsden leave her alone with her prey. Here Newton and his actors were able to reveal Shaw's poetic poignancy to advantage, and old canards about Shaw's lack of heart were eliminated in the intimacy, force, and sensitivity of the performance. Tanner intends to assault Ann's hypocrisy, but she quickly deflects this attack by acting coy and vulnerable. (The high-backed chairs provided Kate Trotter with an effective means of hiding when Ann *pretended* shy discomfort.) Very quickly Ann turns the dialogue to the past and to the moment when Tanner's moral passion was born. She tries to guide Tanner into an open declaration of his stirrings, giving signs of her own genuine romantic attraction towards him - signs that he foolishly overlooks.

Ann understands Tanner's devotion to his own childhood - a time of pastoral happiness when the two of them had enjoyed a special compact. But even then, as Tanner knew of her diabolical cleverness at getting through a boy's guard and "surprising his inmost secrets," he had failed to recognize her love for him. She had coaxed him into divulging his secrets without actually divulging her own. She had known his weakness and played on it rather devilishly for her own satisfaction. And now Tanner, with that recollection bearing upon him, confesses his capitulation to her sly psychological manipulation, but analyzes it as a "bravado: passionless and therefore unreal." This is an amazing confession from a man who normally masks his heart with words about philosophy. And it also brings in his story about an aborted love affair with a girl named Rachel Rosetree (the "rose" in the name is apposite to Ann, as will be shown later). It was, indeed, Ann who had helped thwart that affair, and this had prompted Tanner to develop moral passion in place of a romantic one.

Now the dialogue turns to the implications of his change. Where he sees only with philosophic or scientific eyes, she provokes him into seeing the very passion he has been always avoiding. "You were beginning to be a man, and I to be a woman," she declares. For a brief moment it appears that Tanner recognizes that the two were "beginning to be something more." He equates "the beginning of manhood and womanhood" with "the beginning of love," and even admits that "love began long before that for me. Love played its part in the earliest dreams and follies and romances I can remember." But, then, he spoils the moment for Ann by turning the issue of love into one of moral passion.

Kate Trotter's acting of this scene - usually passed over very lightly by literary and theatre critics - helped Newton give the play its due weight as a sexual comedy. Though her charm and sweetness were more an acquired manner than an organic expression of her being, Trotter imbued her duet with Michael Ball with the kind of controlled romanticism that heightened her appetite and intensity. Her sharpness and brutality were, perhaps, not as strong as they could have been, but this toning-down actually helped in making Ann a quivering human being rather than a coquettish, ruthlessly determined Shavian symbol. And Trotter helped to make Ann far less hypocritical than she is usually made by an actress. This was not a gratuitous act of interpretation, for Shaw carefully reveals that Ann really wishes to have Tanner see her true desires. When she says, "I am never hypocritical with you, Jack," she is not being disingenuous. She adds correctly: "If you and Tavy choose to be stupid about me, that is not my fault." She cannot help the fact that Tanner is a boy at heart who is "frightfully self-conscious," and who turns to destruction (by rhetoric and moral passion) as a subconscious evasion of his true self.

Trotter's performance managed to mediate the two main aspects of Ann's self: the cunning coquette and the genuine soul-mate of a man in need of the very love that frightened him. The first aspect was shown by her pretence at flustered annoyance ("One never knows how to take you"), or by her darting behind Ramsden's desk and then downstage to her boa on "So it was only your vanity that made you run away from us after all?" The feather boa is Shaw's metaphor for the serpentine coils of his predatory woman: it signifies the woman as Life Force, and it animates Ann by its symbolic spirit. Trotter trailed the boa behind her or slowly swung it about with a hint of dangerous mischief. With Ball's Tanner now more firmly in her grasp, she withdrew the boa with a mischievous snicker, and used her own arms to coil around his neck: "I suppose what you really meant by the boa constrictor was this." Her "magnificent audacity" and "devilish charm" (Tanner's phrases) were compounded by her exploitation of Ball's comic nervousness and tenderness. She was able, then, to link the two aspects of Ann's self, making it seem that Tanner was the sly flirt always offending others without really meaning to let go his hold of them.

At this point Trotter's Ann re-established a formal control of the scene, retracting from what could have been a headlong rush of romantic passion had Tanner dropped his defences and other characters not reappeared. This Ann provided the climactic thunderclap for Act I, for as Violet reveals, Ann has known her friend's secret all along. In retreating behind the high-backed chairs, the men made their collective ignominy seem complete.

Act II is a change of setting. We move from Ramsden's London study to an arcadian landscape where, as Newton pointed out in his programme note, "Tanner's car, like his ability to see the obvious, has broken down." One small arch suggested a great iron gate at the bottom of a drive in a large park. This is the act in which we encounter Henry Straker, Tanner's young chauffeur, "a very momentous social phenomenon" as a representative of the New Man - one who "knows the world well from its seamy side" and who exercises a reverse snobbery. As Tanner puts it: "Oh, if you could only see into Enry's soul, the depth of his contempt for a gentleman, the arrogance of his pride in being an engineer, would appal you." The car, in three-quarter actual size, was a toy to both characters - an emblem of Straker's preoccupation with modern technology, and the vehicle of Tanner's panic-stricken flight from the stalking Ann.

Like Ann's boa in Act I, the car helps propel the action, though the two props are markedly different in their symbolic significance. Ann's boa, as Charles A. Berst points out, represents the "instinctive, feminine, serpent-like qualities" of Life Force Woman and is a spirit "as old as the Fall," whereas the car "symbolizes man's escape from vital instincts, and introduces a radically new age." (Leary 61) As Berst's comments are pertinent to any consideration of Shaw's symbolic props, it is useful to quote him at length on the car:

> It is the first stage appearance in any drama of the most ubiquitous workhorse of the twentieth century, a popular culmination of the masculine genius of the Industrial Revolution, a household god giving modern man new mobility, power, speed, and a vicarious sense of virility. Appropriately, along with the car - almost as an adjunct to it - comes the New Man, Henry Straker, the driver-mechanic-engineer who works, repairs, lives by, and worships the machine. Further, it signals a social revolution in which machines and servants have become masters. (Leary 61)

Dominating downstage left of an essentially green and blue décor, it was the magic contraption to conduct Tanner on his journey into the Sierra, and, consequently, into his dream vision of Hell. Already the colours and textures of the design were evidence of a new surrealism. There was a light, fantastical quality - a pastel or colour pencil world instead of a heavily painted one, a world reminiscent of Magritte with its heavenly blue sky and fleecy white clouds.

Kochergin's costume design, rendered in collaboration with his wife, Inna Gabai, complemented the surrealism by its strange un-Englishness, an eerie feeling of displacement. All inspired by the 1911 Sears catalogue, a copy of which existed in Leningrad, they had a slightly odd look, as if there had been some superimposition of symbolic imagination over a very banal reality - particularly in Act I. This gave the play some of its surrealism, in keeping with Newton's conception of a movement through time and space, magical places and seasons.

Apart from the emblematic significance of the setting and car, Act II does not bring any new strokes to the sex comedy. Ann acts in marked contrast to Violet, who values money and comfort over romance and true adventure. Tanner once again reveals himself as someone hoodwinked by Ann. Although he is correct in branding Octavius a "maudlin idiot," he is dead wrong in thinking that the sentimentalist is "the pursued, the marked down quarry, the destined prey." Shaw plays up Tanner's comic pompousness simply to offset it by the character's stunning misreading of Ann's true intent. A more subtle note, however, is Shaw's deployment of the Don Juan motif. Tanner calls Octavius "the real descendant of Don Juan" for having been marked by Ann for her own. This from the mouth of one who, in the first act, was already revealed to be in flight from sexual passion and commitment! Even when a note from Rhoda shows that Ann has schemed to have Tanner left all to herself, the revolutionist fails to catch on. His verbosity in this act becomes what Shaw terms a "sociological rage" as he caricatures women and marriage, and he does not see the comic irony in his advice to Ann to be her own emancipationist. When he invites her for a car-ride, he never for a moment expects her to agree. When she does, he is panic-stricken, and the car becomes his vehicle of escape - set to a piano flourish in Newton's production.

The brevity of this act - it runs twenty-nine minutes - and the abrupt conclusion hardly prepare us for the total change of mood and style in Act III. At the end of the pastoral interlude, the hero has run away, and the romantic love-chase begun in earnest. Suddenly we find ourselves in a camp of political brigands in the Spanish mountains. "Fantasy has now completely overtaken the plot," remarked Newton in his programme note, and Kochergin's design aided and abetted the fantasy. There was the most enchanting fairy-tale composition of brown, purple, green, and blue. Cultivated patches of vegetation were suggested by the green-lit floor, and tall stone peaks and precipice were conveyed in the fastidious shadings of the rock projections on two arches. There was economy instead of profusion, magnificent control instead of wild nature, and yet there was a storybook magic to the scene, achieved in large part by Robert Thomson's superb lighting that modulated from dusky shadows to bewitching white dissolves for the *Don Juan in Hell* sequence.

The two dominant emblems at the outset were the brigands' campfire and Mendoza's carriage. The brigands sat around the fire, arguing most comically about the differences between anarchists and social democrats, and the fire, which lent suggestions of heat and passion, prefigured the red and black colours of the dream sequence. Mendoza's carriage to just right of centre-stage was a black emblem of his mystery and a very practical device for his entrances, exits, and costume-changes. It was also a counter to Tanner's car, especially as its dark, mysterious doors admitted us to no interior, and the broken coach, with its high wheels and curious lines, was slightly disturbing in the enchantment of the Sierras. Like some of the costumes, it had a Russian source, for it was modelled after an engraving, in the St. Petersburg equivalent of the *Illustrated London News*, of the coach in which Czar Alexander II had been assassinated.

The element of mystery was most pronounced in this act, beginning with the carriage and continuing with the extraordinary collection of Mendoza's followers. Mendoza himself was in black with a red ascot and looked like a suavely affected chieftain (a fitting precursor for Mephistopheles). His band was cunningly eclectic and included a Frenchman, a goatherd, a Spanish officer, an English and a German socialist, and three other members, all unified in their roles as attendants, but all in distinct dress and manner.

Shaw balances satire against fantasy, starting with a burlesque of anarchists and social democrats, continuing with the contrasting epigrammatic wit of Mendoza and Tanner - especially in their introduction where the chieftain announces loftily that he is a brigand who lives by robbing the rich, while Tanner promptly retorts that he is a gentleman who lives by robbing the poor - and culminating in Straker's consternation at Mendoza's awful love doggerel about Louisa, Straker's sister. The surrealism lies in the concatenation of comic incongruities: a love-sick Spanish brigand who yearns to be an Englishman (though Barry MacGregor was clearly far more English than Spanish), bandits who have learned their business from an American train-robber, a chauffeur's sister whose intellect reaches "forward into the twentieth century" while her social prejudices reach "back into the dark ages," and an English revolutionist who is about to share a very strange dream with the bandit.

"This is a strange country for dreams," pronounces Mendoza, and the portentousness of his statement was borne out of successive happenings, all of which accentuated Shaw's surrealism as a heightened translation of dream reality into an operatic one, with the main Edwardian figures metamorphosing into Mozartian characters, but with Mendoza and his band transformed into a distinctly different order of beings.

Shaw's script calls for a stillness to settle and darkness to deepen as the stars dim and vanish, and the sky "seems to steal away out of the universe. Instead of the Sierra there is nothing: omnipresent nothing. No sky, no peaks, no light, no sound, no time nor space, utter void." The script also calls for a ghostly Mozartian strain and a visual transition to the sixteenth or seventeenth century. Newton's production, however, created its own aural and visual effects. Tanner stumbled in a blue, smoky darkness, not knowing where he was. He could have been in some mysterious holding-zone, as it were, between the real world and a surreal one. There was an other-worldly background music, for which Christopher Donison had used electronic sounds and voices, mixed with one of the themes from *Don Giovanni*, which blended with the solitary offstage soprano's falling theme that held a low note for a good five to ten seconds. The music grew unhinged and ungrounded, and the lighting bewitched by its virtuosity.

Time and space suddenly seemed to expand and become as one as the evening glow became nocturnally umbral, and then all colour appeared to dissolve and become white. Stillness led to an unfathomable stealing away of sky - as if out of the universe. Instead of the Sierra, there was nothing but a void - a void suggested by an unearthly pallor and ghostly music. Then with sudden brief explosions of light (like flashbulbs popping), there were swirls of mist, and characters mysteriously appeared out of some strange hallucination.

There was a trio, faintly recognizable in the blue penumbra, as leading figures from *Don Giovanni*: an old woman (Dona Ana at seventy-seven), Don Juan, and the Statue. Kate Trotter's scratchy voice lost characterization, but did not reduce the didactic point of this brief interlude before the Devil's appearance. The deliberate unreality of characters transformed into operatic counterparts emphasized the super-reality of the hell sequence. With the "humbug" of death, age, and change dropped, the Mozartian characters could lead us into a fantastical dialogue about the meanings of life, art and eternity.

The brief interlude (with Dona Ana, the Statue, and Don Juan, all introduced by spotlights and with the Statue given a trombone accompaniment) shifts Shaw's appeal from the visual to the aural, but Newton stressed all the possible connections between the symbolic figures of the hell fantasia and their Edwardian descendants. For one thing, the sex comedy was continued with Ana's duelling with Don Juan, and with the latter's professed boredom with any cultivation of love and beauty. For another, the Tanner who, by the end of the second act is torn by contrary impulses, doubts, and fears, metamorphoses in his own dream into a Don Juan who has found no particular happiness in pleasure, who is bored with the eternal amusements of Hell, and who is yearning to find his way to Heaven where he will devote himself to contemplation of love and beauty.

Ann Whitefield has turned into Dona Ana because "Wherever ladies are is hell." In Hell she can still pursue her Tanner/Don Juan, though she is no match intellectually for him or the Devil (a sentimental Mendoza become a sentimental demon). True to her nature as Everywoman, however, she is in quest of fulfilling her destiny as a potential mother - the possible creator of the Superman. But she clearly belongs to neither Heaven nor Hell - rather like the Statue.

The dialogue in Hell is obviously meant to be read metaphorically, with the argument becoming an elaborate extension of the psycho-sexual struggle between Ann and Jack. The Life Force, which controls both characters, is propagated through the lengthy discussion (almost ninety minutes long on stage), and even though the Devil makes a strong romantic case for a sensual life (as Tanner makes a witty one for intellectual life), it is the Life Force which ultimately resolves the philosophical and sexual comedy.

The production created a marvellous stage idiom to turn reality both upside down and inside out. Kochergin's setting and Thomson's lighting provided additional energy to complement the dialogue's vitality. Mozart in the background yielded to jazz and quasi-funk (with Joe Cocker mixed in), for eternity was projected as a continuum that blends all epochs into one. The campfire disappeared and so did the carriage, as a long banquet table slid forth from the darkness to a larger-than-life orchestration that was almost Wagnerian in the harmonic vocabulary. An ominous sense of uncertainty and expectation was created. The table was all white, red, and gold, with candles, silverware, and decorations. Mendoza and his attendants - now the Devil and his Satanic guests -were resplendent in formal evening wear as they jiggled and danced. The arches now projected red and white swags with a parrot as insignia, perhaps representative of birds trapped in an infernal gilded cage or, possibly, reversing the crow image of the characters in Act I. This was the Hell of eternal sensual indulgence, exquisitely well-mannered demons, hot music, but, ultimately, champagne boredom and inertia. Evidently taking his cue from Mendoza's earlier career as a waiter at the Savoy Hotel, Newton and Kochergin presented a marvellous conceit for the play-within-a-play. Instead of an underworld with links to pantomime and the Demon King, Newton and Kochergin devised a Grand Hotel operated by the Devil - "one of those awful grand hotels," explains Cameron Porteous, "where you have everything you want and you're bored out of your head because you do nothing."

One of the chief problems for a designer is to link the first two acts and the conclusion to the Don Juan debate-oratorio. Kochergin resolved the problem by his reverse emblem of the rose. What would become a clear symbol by the end of the play was here prefigured by a gold rose - an emblem for Ann's sensuality and Tanner's awkward chivalry, as well as an inversion of the idea of Hell, as a place of pain. The gold rose showed that Hell, contrary to puritan propaganda, was an illusion of pleasure.

With a very simple series of planes, the set design evoked a palpable atmosphere, preserving some of the Magritte qualities but with the surrealistic touches that heightened the symbolism of the play-within-a-play. Newton clearly suggested that it was not simply Tanner's dream, but everyone's shared reverie. Roebuck Ramsden and Ann had fallen asleep in the car in the mountains, and they had become part of the dream, for Ann turned into Dona Ana who had married Octavius and shrivelled up.

The unity of the main play and the Don Juan in Hell sequence depends on "Tanner's identification of Ann with Woman and Woman with Will. In the dream of hell (where there is no objective reality, only subjectivity), Jack's comic fear of Ann is projected in Juan's cosmic vision of a Will greater than his own." (Morgan 107) But what would have been a mere Morality play or debate about and among allegorical abstractions became, with Shaw's art and Newton's direction, a metaphorical struggle between the two sexes to justify their destinies, as well as a struggle between those who would wish to understand nature and others who merely submit cynically to it.

The Don Juan in Hell sequence is rhetorical art at its most eloquent, but even though it can be a pleasure to hear in itself, it is a difficult challenge for actors. Shaw's concern is with "the evolving mind's eye and its higher plane of vision which should enable us to see 'the purpose of Life.' His intellect sets the stage; his fervor and his wit light it. What absorbs his attention and ours is not a place but the plight of Man." (Brown 131) Fine ideas, but how can they be made theatrically absorbing in the context of an Edwardian comedy? A great debate is great stuff for a platform reading, but what can happen to the elaborate fantastical metaphor that Shaw has created in the text?

Newton's solution was to relegate Mozart, Nietzsche, Schopenhauer, and Wagner to Heaven (where they could presumably debate eternally the reality of life and art), while cleverly continuing to balance visual satire and fantasy against high-flown debate. A high comic tone was established from the first with the formally accoutered devils in their black tails applauding the Devil as he emerged from his carriage. This immediately set up expectations of a polemical entertainment without divorcing the speakers from their earlier incarnations in the play proper. The minor devils, by their polite applause and concentrated listening, directed their energy towards Barry MacGregor's suave figure, and helped draw the audience's focus to the Devil on his key arias. Newton alternated between stasis and movement, with the Devil, Don Juan, and the Statue allowed to move upstage or down, left or right of centre, or even sit still for stretches, so long as the stationing, grouping, or choreography did not detract from a specific purpose. Moreover, he did not treat the long passages as technical set-pieces, but directed his leads to take the proceedings as a comedy about the nature, scope, and manifest purpose of the Life Force.

Given the considerable craft and experience of Michael Ball, William Hutt, and Barry MacGregor, the Hell sequence gained in colour, wit, and vitality what it downplayed in vocal music. The actors made the dialogue sound impromptu rather than premeditated and rehearsed, with particular grace-notes struck by MacGregor's sophisticated and confident self-indulgence, Ball's epigrammatic pithiness, and Hutt's "military habits of speech" and mystification at abstract thought. Every joke was pinned, every important didactic point hit in the repartée, and every male character given his due. And when Don Juan opted for Heaven over Hell, the staging culminated in Ann's cry for her work yet to be done, and a final dance of devils (this time to funk music) as the long banquet table quickly retreated in smoke. The dancing devils popped in and out of view from behind the central arch, which then took on the Sierra rock texture as the lighting changed.

The offstage soprano and piano returned, but now the song represented light flooding into a previously unlit world. Newton and Donison both recognized the connection of light to the Life Force - as in some religions - and the song had a beautiful, warm, radiant quality. It was dawn, and we were returned to the cave site where the dreamers had obviously awakened from a shared dream. The surrealism of the Hell sequence dissolved into a strange realism, as the in-coming party of Ann, Violet, Hector, and Ramsden, in long capes, veils or goggles, looked like bizarre creatures from an alien world.

The transitional music to Act IV was provided again by voice and piano, but this time in a slightly flippant manner. Shaw's text is dense and has a spoken music all its own, so Newton and Donison did not use any more accompaniment until the end.

In the final two sets of décor, we were given a garden in Grenada and an even warmer scene with a camera on tripod and then a beautiful red rose projected between the arches. The camera was a concrete means of delivering Newton's metaphor of illusion, for it was meant to suggest that it was the audience that was being photographed. The metaphor had an epistemological significance, for one of the questions prompted by the prop was: Whom were we watching - the characters alone, or reflections of ourselves? Now it became clear that the arches were supposed to represent the bellows of an old-fashioned camera, and that this production was all along designed to question the reality behind the images.

The dusty, warm colours of green, orange, and yellow marked the movement into a pastoral clime, where hypocrisy was supposed to be unveiled, inhibitions finally cast off, and truths of the Life Force and of human nature consolidated as universalities. The only discordant note in the composition was the senior Malone, a frank capitalist with an eye and a pocketbook for buying up whatever he wished. Significantly, he was the only figure in black - a dark figure in a bright garden.

Although Al Kozlik strained credibility with his false Irish accent, he did not obscure Shaw's crisp satire on pragmatism. Malone threatens to cut off Hector's financial support if his son marries Violet, but the tycoon discovers more than his match in Violet, who believes in having money without having to work for it. She charms the old man into her sway. Shaw presents her as a version in a different key of Ann Whitefield: she is, as Ann proclaims, "as hard as nails," and she gets her own way "without coaxing - without having to make people sentimental about her." She ends the sparring between Malone *fils* and Malone *père* by shrewd sophistry. Patrick Masurkevitch could do nothing with the psychological side of Hector, and his strained, sometimes hoarse voice merely grated on a spectator's ears, but Kozlik, apart from his accent, did accentuate the senior Malone's motive for retribution against the English society that had impoverished and humiliated him and his fellow Irish. His worldly-wise feistiness is tamed, however, by Violet. It is Woman who gets the upper-hand, in keeping with the will of the Life Force. Pity was that Julie Stewart lacked colour and haughty crispness for Violet, though she did not scant the character's pride and intelligence.

The final act must move somehow to the inevitable conclusion of Tanner's submission to Ann, but before this climactic event there is the small, though significant matter of Octavius' unrequited yearning after Ann. Newton groomed Kate Trotter to be the very personification of subtle sophistry. When her Ann claimed that Tanner did not know his own mind, and that her parents had willed her to marry Jack, Krantz's Octavius had no option but to admire her "unselfish" disposition. Then Trotter launched into her skilful disarming of Octavius by charming him into giving her up. How sincerely she described Octavius' predicament as a romantic poet with illusion in his eyes, yet how forcefully she dismissed his momentary desperation, offering a hard-grained witty consolation: "A broken heart is a very pleasant complaint for a man in London if he has a comfortable income." With Octavius' defences laid down, she lit up with "mischievous ecstasy" (in Shaw's phrase) over the imminent prospect of Jack's submission: "Theres no such thing as a willing man when you really go for him." Jennifer Phipps made delightful work with Mrs. Whitefield's consternation, but how wrong this mother was about her daughter!

Set for the ultimate encounter between Ann and Jack, the production moved into an area of psychosexual intimacy that is rarely experienced in Shavian theatre. The scene between the two lasts a mere nine minutes of acting time, but Newton and his duo worked with a strong palette of emotional colouration. Ann begins with a quiet suggestion that Tanner ought to get married, bringing forth a quick explosion in his instant recognition of her stratagem. Ann is placidly playful, while Tanner is exasperated at having to do the world's will and not his own. He tries pleading in bemusement and then launches a witty diatribe against marriage. She accuses him of flattering her simply because he intends marriage. Their duet of accusation and counter-accusation is a strangely fascinating courtship ritual, with the outcome now not in any doubt, for the unwilling is obviously ensnared by the unconscionable. Tanner is too plainly in the grip of the Life Force, and though he has scoffed at Octavius for his poetic temperament that "sees nothing in nature but romantic scenery for love duets," Tanner is himself a victim of his own barren temperament as a philosopher who sees nothing in nature but occasions for rhetoric, even as nature is conspiring to sabotage his rhetoric.

The scene is a bizarre seduction, in which the despairing victim is palpably rendered helpless by what seems to him to be a super-real force. Newton's blocking underscored the precise moment when Tanner recognizes the magic that is defeating him. After he has realized "The trap was laid from the beginning," his statement is expanded by Ann's "From the beginning - from our childhood -for both of us - by the Life Force." And it was on the phrase "Life Force" that Kate Trotter held out her upstage right hand to Michael Ball who discovered that his left hand felt obliged to respond. As his Tanner objected that he would not marry her, the actor moved slowly downstage to Ann during an attempt to resist her magnetic pull. The two met on Ann's line "That is all," falling into a passionate embrace the instant Tanner dropped his resistance to the idea that he loves Ann. The passion was deepened by the anomalies of Tanner's being: on the one hand, a struggle for honour and autonomy; on the other, an enchantment of love for Ann. Both performers projected the pain of love's sudden release, breaking their embrace briefly, only to clasp each other in desperate ardour. Shaw's text is heightened rhetoric at this moment, but there is a whole ocean of yearning below the phrases:

TANNER. If we two stood now on the edge of a precipice, I would hold you tight and jump.

ANN [*panting, failing more and more under the strain*] Jack: let me go. I have dared so frightfully - it is lasting longer than I thought. Let me go: I cant bear it.

TANNER. Nor I. Let it kill us.

Trotter's Ann was clearly at the end of her voluptuous wiles as she yelled: "I am at the end of my forces. I dont care." Then she sank into a half-faint, and for once what could have been a crafty affectation seemed like a genuine reaction to a spontaneous and overpowering impulse - something quite beyond her premeditation or cunning. In fact, it was suggestive of a sexual orgasm, with both her and Tanner panting and gasping with excitement and exhaustion.

With Ann's half-faint, the rest was a brief dénouement, as the others arrived for the ending. The final décor was meant to suggest a rich heat with yellow and orange tints, but the colours were rather washed out in the production. There was no mistaking the sense of the radical changes in the attitudes of the principal characters, all of whom, after all, had made an eventful journey. Summer had broken out for the warm glow of the dénouement. Violet had both her man and her inheritance; Octavius had resigned himself to being broken-hearted over Ann; Ramsden had finally become less choleric over Tanner, though William Hutt made the old reactionary sound defeated. Tanner himself tries to reverse the course of events by launching into yet another aria - this one denying the truth of his happiness, but as the words cascade forth, Ann is merely delighted at the distribution of forces. She has won what she had always set out to win, while Tanner can do nothing more than talk! As Trotter moved slowly towards Ball, with hysterical nervousness and ecstasy, the invisible offstage singer resumed her wordless song, and a large red rose - obviously a metamorphosis of the gold one in the Don Juan In Hell sequence - dominated the rear centre portal.

The red rose sealed this exceptional romantic mood, suggesting by its petals and colour the sexual force (once obscured, even denied) that fused the two lovers. The Tristan-Isolde vibrations in Tanner's words ("If we two stood now on the edge of a precipice, I would hold you tight and jump'') fused something else: the chivalric dawning in Tanner and his essential passion. Finally, the rose crystallized the catharsis of the two lovers. Their secret passion for each other now expressed itself openly by their tears, laughter, and talk. They had purified themselves of all the rubbish of their conventional world and earlier verbal duels. Now their hearts were nakedly exposed to each other, and the rose displaced memories of Tanner's cynical wit and Ann's strategic hypocrisy. The rose was more than romantic decoration for a love duet; it was a link to that earlier garden of childhood in which Tanner and Ann had flirted with each other, unsuspecting then that love could play its part in their earliest dreams and follies and romances.

CHAPTER NINE

MISALLIANCE
(1990)

The first and the last thing I remember from three viewings of the 1990 *Misalliance* is its set design by Leslie Frankish on the long, deep Festival Theatre stage. It was obvious that Newton had performed a major act of reinterpretation on what has often been considered an entertaining but messy comedy. At first glance, the décor seemed to be messy and unfocussed, just what the earliest critics of the play had said of the plot. As in his first version of the play ten years earlier, Newton showed that *Misalliance* was not simply about children and parents; rather, it was a fascinating allegory of a jungle of conflicting ideas and emotions, from whose tangle emerged the powerful image of the modern century with significant changes in thought and behaviour. As was his wont, Newton had seized upon a vivid visual metphor for the play, but this time - unlike in his *Saint Joan, You Never Can Tell*, or *Man and Superman* - he had gone for something lush and florid in décor, with a surrealistic intent.

Taking his cue from the fact that Shaw's great plays - the ones I have made the focus of this book - are not tracts or simple illustrations of ideas, but are really about a profusion of things, Newton and his designer produced a remarkably innovative stage picture that became, in effect, more than a setting: it was virtually another character. In his souvenir programme note, he explained the significance of the décor:

'A glass pavilion commanding the garden' - this is the basic
set for *Misalliance*. An audience before the First World War

would have understood the nuances of the chairs, the taste behind the Viennese pottery. All the little things that Shaw describes would have a richness of meaning. For us these meanings are recondite and particular. (What is the difference between Heals and Maples?) But what we can see is the possibility of connecting the room with what has passed and what is to come. The greater the play, the deeper it digs into its own time and the wider the implications.

The fragile glass pavilion has, for us, become a structure like the Crystal Palace - something that started as a celebration of new ideas but which, by the early twentieth century, has become overgrown, entangled with so many ideas that people are losing their way in the profusion. Tarleton tries to connect everything but he gets lost in this luxuriant abundance. There are strong options - dozens of them - but there is no sense of direction here. The vines and palm trees proliferate. Here's a potted bromeliad called Tennyson, a fern called Darwin, an immense flowering shrub called Ibsen, a pineapple called Marx. Who and what will survive in this intellectual riot in which the family lives?

Into this jungle come two mythic characters who have the ability to cut through the mess. Here are two people, quite terrifying at first sight, one of whom (Lina) has a very special sense of direction. The other (Joey Percival) is in some way as lost as the family, but he carries within him the ability to escape. (There is something mythic about Joey. Before he even arrives he is built up as a god-like figure with three fathers.) And this is 1909. The visitors arrive in the most extraordinary invention - the airplane. It is almost as if today two visitors were to drop by in a private space shuttle. A classic message has arrived not in the last act, but at the end of the first.

Misalliance starts slowly, as if the whole of the nineteenth century - terrifying, glorious, expansionist, and now entangled in its own explorations - has for a moment taken a breath, paused. Wonderful, entertaining ideas about business, growing up, desire, the social structure of the Old Empire fill the air like scent from the flowers in the entanglement of vines. Then with the cracking of steam pipes, screams, the sound of an engine high in the air, the twentieth century - an age of political and sexual revolution - crashes in, bringing with it sounds that resemble only one thing: the war that is so inevitably approaching.

This is an extraordinarily prescient play. It sums up
the long afternoon of Edwardian England. Wonderfully
funny, it reaches deep into the heart of its time to shine on
the beginnings of our own.

This was an extraordinary interpretation of a play that is usually
regarded as a discussion comedy. And certainly the mist, darkness, and
eerie electronic score (of the type heard in mystery or thriller films) as a
large crate was slowly hauled onto a scene luxuriant with sub-tropical or
tropical vegetation, and where a maid carried an axe, showed that this was
no typical Edwardian conservatory, but a hothouse of ferns, vines, and
immense flowering shrubs, which made the atmosphere seem steamy.
The first question was whether this décor was overly-ingenious, clever but
strained, vivid but extravagant. And the second was whether the details
would obscure the play and players, especially as not all the audience had
clear sight-lines, and the actors were sometimes deliberately hidden in
shadow and foliage.

Barry MacGregor, who played Tarleton the successful linen-
draper, offered me an actor's perspective:

That was one of the easiest sets I've ever worked on in my
life. I mean that truthfully. It was quite, quite amazing. The
first time we went onto that set, you just felt totally,
completely at home. There was no problem about moving
chairs. I can't describe it - other than it was like an old shoe,
it was like an old coat. I never felt at any time that I was
overpowered by the set as an actor. I had felt [overpowered]
many times at Stratford by some of the costumes in the early
seventies. I mean shit! it took the first act for people to
realize there was somebody inside that thing.

Where the stark emptiness of the stage in *Man and Superman*
required the ensemble to act, so, strangely enough, did the dense
environment for *Misalliance*. As MacGregor put it: "In fact, it made one
want to fill the space as an actor, and not in the demonstrative, rhetorical
kind of old theatrical fashion." MacGregor still marvels at the instant
rapport he felt with his setting. But what about the lushness, the profusion
of the exotic? How does one reconcile these elements with Tarleton of
Tarleton's Underwear in Hindhead, Surrey? Shaw's stage directions
clearly indicate a bright, summery, elegant setting - not the heavy
"violence" of incongruences in Leslie Frankish's design - the dark
shadows and foliage reminiscent of the colours in Africa, India, or the
Caribbean, the mixture of Victorian and Edwardian pottery and architecture,

with the mechanical innovations of the modern century (such as the swing that brings Johnny down onto the stage, or the new Turkish Bath in its crate, or the ceiling fans). MacGregor reminds us that the heaviness and lushness were elements that Newton and Frankish derived from the largest conservatory in Britain and from the Palm House in Kew Gardens. That was the Victorian element; as for the colonial, Newton used material clutter of pottery and plants that showed how Tarleton was able to afford exotic luxuries and imported fashions. The conjunction of styles in the décor became an important screen for Newton's surrealism, for it added a new perspective to a conventional play, and invited the audience to see what was now filtered through the stage metaphor. The clutter also provided opportunities for Robert Thomson's back-lighting and special effects for signal moments; the tangle was so ingeniously designed as to defoliate itself gradually or dramatically at climactic points.

Actually there was less clutter than what first met the eye, for the acting area was really a trisected stage. The centre area, containing an arched doorway (mostly hidden by the foliage), plants, and pavilion furniture, was used by the major characters at more conventional moments, whereas the other two areas (demarcated by large, tiled, circular entryways) were used for segues between entrances and exits, as wandering zones, or for specially isolated effects.

Newton saw the overall action of the play as a slow casting away of an old world and its stifling attitudes through a series of convulsions. But his production began in a deliberately mysterious manner, with dark shadows, eerie music, and the arduous hauling of a huge wooden crate onto an already dense scene. All the initial stage business of servants and movers was wordless, and the lights came up only two pages into the text, well into the brisk clash between Bentley's throwaway wit and Johnny's bullying caddishness. Visually, the casting of tall, lean Duncan Ollerenshaw as Bentley and tall, dark Mark Burgess as Johnny scored points for the comedy, especially as Ollerenshaw was hardly the "little one" that Mrs. Tarleton sought to protect from Johnny's threatened battering, though he was a cowering crybaby when his flamboyant wit and overbred affectation deserted him.

The Tarletons were obviously of (in Bentley's words) the "great and good middle class." The heavy, hybrid materialism of their home made this point scenically, and the family members were clear incarnations of the phrase. Jennifer Phipps' Mrs. Tarleton had a wonderful tête-à-tête with daughter Hypatia on the "nasty, sneering" aristocracy, and although her absurd sense of delicacy and decency gave vent to a comedy of wry manners (with a particularly amusing anecdote concerning her outrage at a certain duchess' conversation about drainage), Phipps did not miss her moments to underline the mother's concern for her precious plants or her misgivings about her husband's boastful philanthropy and commercialism. Helen Taylor's Hypatia, brisk and blonde, was also an amusing pragmatist ("Theres money in underwear: theres none in wild-cat ideas"), though deep, wild passion beat vitally beneath her respectable constraints. Unlike her brother, whose anti-cultural bias compounded his bourgeois vehemence, she was a living paradox: a romantic who seemed to know that even love could be a question of barter. Frustrated by the lack of suitable male wooers, she merely tolerated Bentley ("who else is there?"), but her "knight" would come later. In the meantime, she could only yearn to be "an active verb," protest her brother's bullying of Bentley, and flirt shamelessly with old Lord Summerhays while waiting anxiously for "something to happen." While her father, with his magpie eclecticism and self-fancied wisdom, could meditate on his destiny in the garden, she had no evident destiny as yet.

As foils, father and daughter were splendid. Barry MacGregor sounded bright woodwind notes for Tarleton's bounteous aphorisms, satirising himself as a middle-class Prometheus chained to the "rock" of his drapery shop, while yearning for something that would "give a scope" to all his faculties. In this genial debate with Richard Farrell's Summerhays on the subject of colonial civilization - in which Summerhays holds to an imperialist line - MacGregor built to an absurdly funny climax as he wandered off stage right amid his jungle of vines and ferns, discoursing on his urge to meditate on destiny, and reaching his incongruous climax while completely offstage. "Tarleton meditating on his destiny. Not in a toga. Not in the trappings of the tragedian or the philosopher. In plain coat and trousers: a man like any man." As he exited, his voice trailed off a little. "And beneath that coat and trousers a human soul." Then the voice suddenly soared: "Tarleton's Underwear!"

Helen Taylor's Hypatia achieved her own splendid effect, but hers was done less by vocal virtuosity than by attitude. In her flirtatious duet with Lord Summerhays, she was the incarnation of the Life Force, speaking as if there were a secret destiny to unite the two of them. Taylor's ardour and gay levity rubbed against Farrell's shuddering delicacy and embarrassment ("Stop, Stop. Can no woman understand a man's delicacy?"). Farrell's lower energy and bland exterior worked to his advantage by default, as it were, making him seem very much like an old colonial still looking at life from the window of his club which was stuffed with retired Anglo-Indian Civil Servants. He lack of airs with Hypatia turned their interlude into a ghostly and ghastly sort of romance. Where Taylor was a nymph willing to be wicked and shocking rather than wither into respectability, Farrell was her improbable love-object, too old, too civilized, and too grey to be a satyr.

Taylor's super-abundant vitality (a heightened reflection of her father's) had its showcase in her impassioned protest of a lack of destiny. In this passage, she reached high excitement on the top step, rear centre. She was clearly the Tarleton most prepared for a radical convulsion, and her sincere desire for adventure dropped out of the sky was fulfilled with the sudden noise of an approaching plane. With her cry, the stage filled with rushing members of the household, the lights went off, vines shook violently, pipes burst, steam and music spilled out, and glass shattered at the convulsion of a plane-crash.

Joey Percival - the "mythic" man with three "fathers" - appeared in a pilot's outfit in the middle of these shocks, as a sudden, dazzling, apocalyptic light shone rear centre. Then, with the lights going off again, and the same apocalyptic light beaming briefly, came the second shocking form in aviator's dress. The alarmed shrieks from the Tarleton women increased when it was discovered that the figure was a woman's in man's dress. Tarleton was not alarmed by this incongruity, and as the ceiling fans noisily dispelled the smoke and steam from the burst pipes, his formal introduction of his family and guests to Lina Szczepanowska, the cross-dressed aviatrix, was drowned in the din. Once the thick smoke cleared, the arched pavilion doorway appeared distinctly for the first time in the play. The combination of abrupt lighting changes, portentous sound effects, and startling entrances by Joey and Lina all magnified the wonder of this "magical" phase. By refusing to change her dress, and by incomprehensibly asking for a Bible, six oranges, and a music stand, Lina exerted her "magical personality" - though Sharry Flett lacked vocal authority and charisma to make the "magic" work dynamically. Thunderstruck by her and Percival, Jennifer Phipps' "chickabiddy" scurried about frantically, while Farrell's Summerhays allowed a vague shadow of guilt to pass across his face at a sudden recognition - as yet undisclosed to his company - that Lina might be the Polish acrobat with whom he had once enjoyed a liaison in Vienna. Of the older generation, only MacGregor's Tarleton was positively charmed by Lina's unorthodox lack of conventionality and appetite for danger. Inspired by her free spirit, he wooed her with epigrams formulated by his eclectic reading tastes. But knowing that he was too reliant on books for wisdom, Lina would draw him away to teach him gymnastic exercises for his health. She was, indeed, the "divine spark" too often denied by civilization.

The next significant convulsion came from Simon Bradbury's Gunner, the young, cheaply dressed, nervous little clerk out for revenge against Tarleton for having seduced and abandoned his mother. Once again, as for the abrupt arrival of Percival and Lina, Newton used a startling lighting effect - this time a cue of darkness for Gunner's entrance through the arched doorway. With a gun cocked and with nervous little looks and tense movements, Bradbury stumbled into vines before finding his way into the Turkish Bath once he had heard grass-stained, tattered Hypatia calling for dishevelled and tattered Percival. Then the lights were quickly up for the peculiar love-contest, in which woman was the pursuer and man the pursued. Bradbury's Gunner dropped from sight, except for momentary poppings-up. The comic incongruity, however, of a would-be assassin hiding in a Turkish Bath in an English country-home and compelled to eavesdrop on an unusual sex game, was not of particular force, perhaps because Bradbury's entrance had not been particularly grotesque in its comedy. Usually a hyperkinetic actor given to excessive business, Bradbury did not create an extraordinary first impression. He opted to play a hapless gunman, bullied all too easily by the intimidating array of figures from a world quite above his own.

Shaw's themes of intimidation and submissiveness were borne out of the Gunner-Hypatia-Percival section, first in the very unorthodox sex game dominated by Hypatia, and second in the subsequent action involving Gunner and the main ensemble. Despite her sexual passion and racing romantic vitality, in and out of the woods and heather, Hypatia is the very daughter of a domineering class. She strikes Percival across the face when she feels the chill of his prudent reluctance to act upon the moment. She dislikes the fact that he, being "too well brought up," is unprepared to cast off the tight corset of his social bond, electing a good, stiff conventionality instead of a real, spontaneous freedom. Her sexual and emotional dominance are shocks to Gunner, as, indeed, they would be to any conventional Victorian or Edwardian reared on gender stereotypes and social proprieties.

But other shocks come from the bullying habits of the males. Unable to generate a tragic intensity by his declaration of murderous intent, Gunner, who reveals himself to be the illegitimate son of Tarleton, is treated scornfully. Not quite in the right key for Gunner's bathos ("I am the son of Lucinda Titmus. She is dead. Dead, my God! and you are alive"), Bradbury did not transcend a stock lugubriosness mixed with mock-heroic socialist fervour. His upraised arms in salute for "Hindhead's turn will come!" were funny enough, but it was really left to Barry MacGregor's Tarleton to carry off the comedy. Shaw's "tragic" little cashier is made comic by his yearning for an unlikely revenge and political revoltuion. But there is equal comedy in Tarleton's peppery chatter that suddenly turns into anger when the shopkeeper realizes that he has been sponsoring Free Libraries for the likes of Gunner.

Lina quickly disarms Gunner, but then out of pity for him, she offers to take him to a gymnasium and turn him into a real man. There was a nice little touch of comic mayhem with Flett's Lina and MacGregor's Tarleton pulling Gunner by his arms in opposite directions, thereby threatening dismemberment in addition to subjugation. Shaw builds a context of comic anarchy, in which Gunner is thoroughly confused by violent shifts in his fortune. Physically manhandled at one moment and insulted at another, he finds himself alone in hostile company where he is forced to recant for having impeached Hypatia's character by reporting on her wildcat behaviour. Bradbury read Gunner's formal recantation (dictated by Percival) in a rapid, imcomprehensible whisper, but without much sense of comedy. It was only when Phipps' Mrs. Tarleton turned sympathetic to the "poor orphan," that Bradbury milked the moment by throwing himself on his knees and hugging her around the waist, while she turned her vexation against Percival.

This section concluded with Bentley's being carried off across Lina's back after his lamentation at losing Hypatia. In the midst of all the commotion, there was a subtle note: MacGregor's Tarleton was observed wearing a little less clothing. Without jacket or cape and with his shirt-sleeves rolled up above the elbow, he was a physical emblem of reduced conventionality, though he was by no means the first or last one on stage who had subtly modified his appearance. Bentley had doffed his jacket after his enforced visit to the gymnasium in Lina's company, and Mrs. Tarleton had earlier removed her *écru* shawl and *écru* celery-striped jacket. But Tarleton's informality was more dramatically noticeable. By becoming less formal in his clothing, he seemed to be gradually drawing himself away from the role of a self-conscious, respectable shop-keeper with pretensions to culture and social-climbing.

As the action wore one, even the décor grew less burdened by prop dressings. There were fewer vines and more back-lighting, as though confusion had lessened with the dawning of wisdom. A turquoise sky glowed warmly for the final act. The house was obviously heated up by the "mythic" Percival and Lina, and the dense clutter of Edwardian ideology was being stripped away in the face of the future. Superficial respectability was sloughed off by several characters. Hypatia was clearly no average lady in her indecorous pursuit of Percival who, in turn, was hardly a true gentleman in his bullying of Gunner. And Lord Summerhays, though decent enough in appearance and speech, approved of fraud and force when law and gentle persuasion did not work to advantage.

Newton's vision of the play was one of a comedy in which divine sparks are set off in the stuffy ambience of English respectability. The "magic" of the play was re-emphasized by Gunner's Dionysiac drunkenness - an attack that found Simon Bradbury, inebriated with sloe gin and Mrs. Tarleton's sympathy, stomping over plants, knocking down pots, and gushing the pugnacious rhetoric of a fervid manhood. The "magic" was also underscored by Percival's description of the woods, for which Thomson's lighting glowed an expressionistic pink and blue as Peter Krantz spoke with enchanted wonder. Tarleton, once quite unperturbed by the flurry of strange events, now was bewildered: "How is it going to end?" Once facilely dismissive of Gunner's confusion, he himself felt strangely confused, though he remained vitally curious. Once complacent about his philosophy of education, he was now shaken by Percival's unsentimental criticism of parents and by Hypatia's bold defiance. With cane in hand, MacGregor staggered after wanton Hypatia, registering the wrath of a defeated bourgeois Lear: "You're laughing at me. Serve me right! Parents and children! No man should know his own child. No child should know its own father. Let the family be rooted out of civilization! Let the human race be brought up in institutions!" The tone was one of regretful impotence because he was no longer able to coerce Hypatia into submitting to his wishes.

The stuffiness of the house was visibly shaking apart. Flett's Lina delivered an aria (about the house and its unhealthy obsessions) as she stood on a step that put her above all others - except Johnny who, true to his nature, confused romanticism with sound business propositions. This was meant to be her greatest rhetorical moment, but although Flett offered an intelligent reading, her lack of vocal power and technical virtuosity did not exploit the rich possibilities of Lina's thrilling independence. Lina's speech is an expression of a disciplined aesthetic - its purposeful phrasings, though reminiscent of a schoolmistress's lessons, are catalyzed into fiery execrations. Flett simply lacked the colour and variety to carry off the muscular prose with transcendental charisma. She was beautiful and charming, but her technique, quite adequate for her separate dealings with Tarleton, Johnny, and Lord Summerhays, did not suffice for the glorious climax where her spirit is supposed to soar with a lion-tamer's bravado, a conjurer's power, and an opera singer's allure. Here she was merely vehement, rather than a paradox of beast and deity.

However, Newton's assured direction assisted the text, for as Flett left the stage with Ollerenshaw's trembling Bentley in tow, she slammed the arched door. Immediately, more vines fell away and smoke rose in the background. The *leitmotif* of misalliances - between parents and children, age and youth, rich and poor, appearance and reality, talk and action, body and soul, and, most of all, the characters and the New Age - crystallized in the final positionings. On Mrs. Tarleton's "Is there anything else?" (delivered in bemusement), chimes and music sounded, and darkness grew with the characters' slow movements for their final configuration. With Lord Summerhays down left, Percival and Hypatia off to the right,

Johnny off to the left (the last to be affected by Lina and, so, the last male to be unjacketted), and Mrs. Tarleton given centrestage, MacGregor's Tarleton slowly and unsteadily ascended the steps leading to the arched doorway, and tried to answer his wife's question in broken phrases. He was visibly shaken by the strange wonder of Lina, and as a small flock of birds flew upward past him, the curtain descended on a world of characters largely mismatched with their changing era. All the bullying and intimidation had ceased - at least temporarily - and although it was not clear if England would ever be cleansed of its imperialistic taints, it was clear that the characters had at least confronted the convulsions of the New Age without remaining radically unchanged.

The production was certainly clever, but was it a success? On a conceptual level, yes. However, the contextual density and richness proved distracting to me as I sat through two performances. It seemed to be a case of missing the play for all the trees on stage. Yet when I viewed the archival tape, the smaller geometry of the video screen restricted the distractions and made the staging seem more concentrated and focussed. The tape compelled me to watch the actors and the choreography, and not allow my eye to wander around Leslie Frankish's extravagant set. The décor became an active metaphor, profusely vibrant in spirit, significantly detailed, but not as overpowering and as crowded as it had seemed in the Festival Theatre. In fact, it forced me to watch the play through Newton's peculiar surrealistic screen. The extraordinary design invited meticulous concentration from a viewer, as much as it did larger, concentrated acting from the cast.

This production, then, gave evidence of Newton's continuing risks with Shavian theatre. Whether its particular extravagance will set the scale for Newton's future experiments with Shaw remains to be seen. Based on his record, it is foolish to expect a single, simple path. The only certainty is that he will not use the same metaphor or approach twice, unless he can elaborate or modify a context and a concept in order to provide a unique revelation.

CONCLUSION

Christopher Newton's way of fusing Shaw's Edwardian ambience with his own modernism has produced shockwaves among those academics who prefer not a comma changed or a jot altered in the texts. But Newton has always attempted to present the plays for a modern audience ''without destroying the integrity of the pieces.'' It is admittedly difficult for academics - who are concerned with preserving the integrity of the *writer* - to see that Shaw's plays were meant for performance, and that, in Newton's words, ''anything that's meant for performing goes through a sea-change of some kind.'' Newton would like an audience to be startled out of its complacency about Shaw; he would like it to see with fresh eyes. Earlier generations would not have made the same connections with the plays in quite the same way that our generation does. ''But the words are the same,'' Newton points out. ''They're sort of doing the same things up there. But today we have a different reaction to them. The job of the director, I believe, is not to destroy the integrity of the piece but to make it connect. It's got to connect with a modern audience. If it doesn't connect, then what the hell is the point of doing it?''

In the winter of 1990-91, prior to rehearsals for *The Millionairess*, which he was to direct the following summer, he pondered a viable approach to a play whose quirkiness troubled him. Kenneth Tynan had thought the play ''almost without wit'' and with ''hardly any of those somersaulting paradoxes with which, for so long, Shaw concealed from us the more basic gaps in his knowledge of human behaviour.'' The characters ''talk interminably, infectiously, and almost interchangeably,'' and the play is marked by "a querulous fumbling; the dialogue is twice as noisy as Shaw's best, and roughly half as effective." (Tynan 115-116) However, the heroine, Epifania Ognisanti di Parerga, is a challenge to a star actress, being "the Shavian muse unveiled and magnificently named." (Morgan 326) On reading the script, Newton found it "funny and charming and, more than that, irritating and strange." There were some terrible jokes, and then a bizarre scene with two elderly characters in a sweatshop, as if from another time, place, and play. Newton was perplexed. "Now Shaw was no fool. Shaw was this great man - this man that I had spent my life at the moment promoting. So what's going on? What is going on that I can get hold of and show that it's all part of something?" How, he worried, could he stage it in a way that would be exciting? The irritating part was that suddenly halfway through the first act, he got bored himself. What was he not seeing about the play? He had a suspicion that one way he might be able to stage it was by recognizing that *The Millionairess* is made up of "turns" - like music-hall turns. "I know Shaw didn't put songs into it. But I think maybe one of the ways of getting what he did write across to a modern audience in the *tone* he wanted is to have them, every now and then, break into song. So I'm exploring that at the moment. You may not see that on stage."

I mention this pre-production story simply to make a few points clear about Christopher Newton. First, he does not have sharp, preconceived, dogmatic notions about how a production will take shape. Like Robin Phillips, he is a contextual rather than a conceptual director, which means that he creates a certain environment without ever decreeing absolutely what an actor must do within it. He carries his actors into the text, rather than bending the text to accommodate his actors. Unfortunately, as in *Saint Joan* and parts of both his *Misalliance* productions, his casts are not always up to the challenges. Shavian acting is difficult on its own - as simply a piece of brilliantly orchestrated rhetorical speaking - but when infused by Newton's heightened sense of reality, it requires both superb technique and ample stage experience to gear it to the tone and weight and depth that Newton would like.

Second, he does seek to preserve the integrity of Shaw's text - even tonally - but not as an autonomous creation distinct from the stage. He always seeks to connect text with audience, and to encourage an audience to quest after the sort of revelation he is seeking. Some of his means, however, have been seriously questioned by Shavianists who seek to have directors and actors respect the text to the ultimate, refusing the validity of cuts or alterations, demanding that musical pitch in the spoken voice be respectful of Shaw's intricate prose. The purists would have the actors speak in the way that Alexander Pope once described a spider spinning a web: ''The spider's touch how exquisitely fine!/Feels at each thread, and lives along the line.'' This goes counter to Newton's theatrical grain. His productions are characterized by textual alterations, and they have certainly not been gilded with arias or bravura acting. Sometimes this has resulted in a somewhat dull orchestration - as in the Tent Scene from the 1981 *Saint Joan* - but at other times, the productions have attained a clarity of thought, an emotional intensity of intuitive meaning - as in *Man and Superman*. Newton understands that the architecture of a speech relies on punctuation, grammar, diction, and imagery, but he also knows that its life is governed by an actor's impulses. Consequently, virtuosic elocution need not be built on a purely technical management of stresses or inflexions; it can create its rhythms and colours by an actor's revelation of a character's motivation and meaning. Michael Ball's Tanner, for instance, was hardly a traditionalist interpretation. It never sought to be a cascading display of claptrap epigrams. It was, instead, a flesh-and-blood creation, lumpishly awkward in physical appearance, but intelligently shaped and always pulsing with a vital heartbeat.

Third, Newton looks for a metaphor that summarizes the significance of a play. The designs for *Saint Joan, Heartbreak House, Man and Superman*, and the 1990 *Misalliance* were quite unlike any others for the same plays. Yet they did not make for simply a designer's theatre. Newton does not want a design to be preoccupied with history (a specific period) or with neutral exposition (a setting that makes no point about the play itself). Nor does he seek to make his design exclusive - that is, rigidly referential to its own parameters. His designs set up a metaphor that permits additional meanings, that allows for separate metaphors to co-exist within the production. The 1983 *Caesar and Cleopatra*, for instance, blended op art, ancient history, and more recent European history within its Shadow Box metaphor; the 1985 *Heartbreak House* blended metaphors of dream, nightmare, catastrophe, and magic; the 1989 *Man and Superman* seemed, at times, to encourage a meditation about metatheatre through its camera-bellows image. The old-fashioned camera pointed at the audience in the final act reminded us that it was ultimately the audience and the world outside the play that were being observed and dissected. The minimalism of the design invited us to be critical of the world.

Fourth, in developing his controlling metaphor, Newton provides a new look and feeling to Shaw, and forces an audience to put aside old assumptions and clichés. He often works in moments of silence before the actual spoken text, giving us time to study, accept, and trust his contextual framework. The silence - usually at the opening of a scene - creates a dramatic effect. It underlines the fact that Newton appears to be saying that we should start on a journey of exploration with him from a point of stark, almost empty or naked space, where there is no visible action, no established meaning. The silence allows us to feel part of a dynamic creation, with the director playing Adam to Shaw's Deity, with the actors eventually peopling and filling an imaginative universe with sound and meaning.

The design of a piece is sometimes subtly completed, as it were, by music - as in the cases of *Caesar and Cleopatra*, *You Never Can Tell*, or, best of all, *Man and Superman*. The sense of awe generated by the invisible soprano's song in *Man and Superman* was linked, of course, to the feminine manifestation of the Life Force. The music played a linking role between the various elements of the play that tended to push it in one direction or another - either towards anarchy or surrealism, on the one hand, or towards the familiar and naturalistic, on the other. Because the music was an original soundtrack by Christopher Donison (compounded of elements of Mozart, Wagner, Debussy, Ravel, Joe Cocker, James Brown, and, perhaps, Stephen Sondheim), it was obscure enough to seem other - worldly, yet familiar enough at times to retain a connection with the nineteenth or twentieth century. Consequently, an audience was moved in and out of familiarity, mundanity, and other-worldliness, as if tethered to a helium balloon that only *threatened* to ascend into the ether, without ever fully floating off.

The image of a helium-balloon was actually supplied to me by Christopher Donison, who sees Newton as the balloon-inflater, with the Shavian play as the balloon, the design and/or music, the helium. Implicit in this analogy is the idea of Newton as a dichotomous Edwardian-modernist. Newton plays with different settings for the play, deliberately chooses a mixture of obscure and familiar music, but never steps beyond the parameters that would cut Shaw off from modern relevance *or* the Edwardian age. The textures of his productions may seem quite revolutionary - are, indeed, revolutionary - but the passions are always generated from within the texts themselves. Newton simply releases these feelings from beneath decades of musty, hollow conventionality.

Newton's productions always seem to explore the question: "What *is* Shaw today?" Shaw, of course, was no Shakespeare, in that his genius does not allow for the rich variety of interpretation that Shakespeare's texts do. But he was a much greater playwright than is usually represented on stage. Rather than adhere to the foolish belief that a text speaks for itself, Newton seems to adopt the view that a text is variable - though not as variable as a Tarot pack - and a playing *tradition* no certain guide. As a director, he understands that there is a life not only in the mass and volume of Shaw's words, but in the impulses beneath the words. Often these impulses do not sort with Shaw's overt meaning or intention. On one level, Shaw is not our contemporary. His textual fabric sustains a web of assumptions and attitudes confined to Victorian and Edwardian thinking. Yet, on other levels, Shaw is, indeed, our contemporary, for there is an urge to be provocative and daring that is not to be identified with his specific period alone. Newton, accordingly, keeps his feet on Edwardian soil, while letting his imagination wander into areas where other Shavian directors hardly ever venture. At his best, he is a Shavian revisionist of surrealistic daring. And even when his helium-balloon does not ascend very high, he is at least a New Traditionalist. This is, indeed, a paradox, but then what is Shaw if not a paradox?

BIBLIOGRAPHY

Agate, James. *Red Letter Nights. (A Survey of the Post-Elizabethan Drama in Actual Performance on the London Stage, 1921-1943).* New York/London: Benjamin Blom, 1969.

Alquié, Ferdinand. *The Philosophy of Surrealism.* Trans. Bernard Waldrop. Ann Arbor: The University of Michigan Press, 1965.

Beckerman, Bernard and Siegman, Howard, eds. *On Stage (Selected Theater Reviews from The New York Times 1920-1970).* New York: An Arno Press Book, 1973.

Benson, Eugene and Conolly, L.W., eds. *The Oxford Companion To Canadian Theatre.* Toronto: Oxford University Press, 1989.

Bentley, Eric. *Bernard Shaw* (Amended Edition). A New York: New Directions Paperbook, 1957.

_____. *What Is Theatre? (Incorporating The Dramatic Event).* B New York: Limelight Editions, 1984.

Berst, Charles A. *Bernard Shaw and the Art of Drama.* Urbana: University of Illinois Press, 1973.

Bloom, Harold, ed. *George Bernard Shaw's 'Major Barbara.'* A New York: Chelsea House Publishers, 1988.

_____. *George Bernard Shaw's 'Man and Superman.'* B New York: Chelsea House Publishers, 1987.

_____. *George Bernard Shaw's 'Saint Joan,'* C New York: Chelsea House Publishers, 1987.

Brown, John Mason. *Dramatis Personae. (A Retrospective Show).* New York: The Viking Press, 1965.

Bryden, Ronald with Boyd Neil. *Whittaker's Theatre. (A Critic Looks At Stages In Canada And Thereabouts 1944-1975).* Toronto: University of Toronto Press, 1985.

Chesterton, G.K. *George Bernard Shaw.* New York: Hill and Wang, 1958.

Contemporary Artists (2nd ed.). New York: St. Martin's Press, 1983.

Day, Arthur R. "The Shaw Festival At Niagara-On-The-Lake In Ontario, Canada, 1962-1981: A History." Ph.D. Dissertation, Bowling Green State University, 1982.

Doherty, Brian. *Not Bloody Likely: The Shaw Festival: 1962-1973.* Toronto: J.M. Dent & Sons (Canada) Ltd., 1974.

Dukore, Bernard F. *Bernard Shaw, Playwright. (Aspects of Shavian Drama).* Columbia: University of Missouri Press, 1973.

Evans, T.F., ed. Shaw: *The Critical Heritage.* London: Routledge & Kegan Paul, 1976.

Fergusson, Francis. *The Idea Of A Theater. (A Study of Ten Plays. The Art of Drama In Changing Perspective).* New York: Anchor Books, Princeton University Press, 1953.

Fowlie, Wallace. *Age Of Surrealism.* Bloomington: Indiana University Press, 1963.

Hyman, Ronald. *The First Thrust. (The Chichester Festival Theatre).* London: Davis-Poynter, 1975.

Hill, Holly. *Playing Joan. (Actresses on the Challenge of Shaw's 'Saint Joan')*. New York: Theatre Communications Group, 1987.

Holroyd, Michael. *Bernard Shaw (Volume 1. 1856-1898. The Search for Love.* A London: Chatto & Windus, 1988.

_____, ed. *The Genius of Shaw.* B London: Hodder and Stoughton, 1979.

Irvine, William. *The Universe of G.B.S.* New York: Whittlesey House, 1949.

Kaufmann, R.J., ed. *G.B. Shaw (A Collection of Critical Essays).* Englewood Cliffs, N.J.: Prentice-Hall, Inc., 1965.

Laurence, Dan H. "The Newton Years At The Shaw Festival 1980-89." Address, Cornell University, June 20, 1989.

Leary, Daniel, ed. *Shaw's Plays in Performance. (The Annual of Bernard Shaw Studies, Vol. Three).* University Park and London: The Pennsylvania State University Press, 1983.

MacCarthy, Desmond. *Shaw.* London: Macgibbon & Kee, 1951.

Matthews, J.H. *An Introduction To Surrealism.* Pennsylvania: Pennsylvania State University Press, 1965.

Meisel, Martin. *Shaw And The Nineteenth Century Theater.* New York: Limelight Editions, 1984.

Mills, John A. *Language And Laughter. (Comic Diction in the Plays of Bernard Shaw).* Tucson, Arizona: The University of Arizona Press, 1969.

Morgan, Margery M. *The Shavian Playground. (An Exploration of the Art of George Bernard Shaw).* London: Methuen & Co., Ltd., 1972.

Newton, Christopher. "The Art of Eduard Kochergin" in *Eduard Kochergin: A Poet Of The Stage.* A Published to accompany Kochergin's designs for 'Man and Superman' at the 1989 Shaw Festival, and an exhibition of his stage designs at Rodman Hall, St. Catharines, Ontario. Shaw Festival Theatre, 1989.

_____. Review of *Bernard Shaw: The Search For Love. Vol. 1. 1856-1898* by Michael Holroyd. B Queen's Quarterly, Vol. 97, No. 2 (Summer 1990), 313-314.

O'Doherty, Brian. *The Voice and the Myth. (American Masters)* New York: Universe Books, 1988.

Rosenblood, Norman, ed. *Shaw Seminar Papers - 65.* Toronto: The Copp Clark Publishing Co., 1966.

Rossi, Alfred, ed. *Astonish Us In The Morning. (Tyrone Guthrie Remembered).* London: Hutchinson, 1977.

Shaw, Bernard. *Advice to a Young Critic and Other Letters.* A Intro. E.J. West. New York: Capricorn Books, 1963.

_____. *Four Plays. (With The Author's Notes) Including Candida, The Devil's Disciple, Caesar and Cleopatra,* and *Captain Brassbound's Conversion.* B New York: Dell Publishing Co., Inc., 1965.

_____. *Major Barbara (A Screen Version).* C Baltimore: Penguin Books, 1951.

_____. *Major Critical Essays.* D Intro. Michael Holroyd. Harmondsworth: Penguin Books, 1986.

_____. *Man and Superman.* E Harmondsworth: Penguin Books, 1962.

_____. *'Misalliance' and 'The Fascinating Foundling'.* F Harmondsworth: Penguin Books, 1984.

_____. *Plays Pleasant.* G Harmondsworth: Penguin Books, 1956.

_____. *Plays Political.* Ed. Dan H. Laurence. H Harmondsworth: Penguin Books, 1986.

_____. *Plays Unpleasant.* I Harmondsworth: Penguin Books, 1957.

_____. *The Quintessence of Ibsenism. (Now Completed To The Death Of Ibsen).* J New York: Hill and Wang, 1960.

_____. *Saint Joan.* K Harmondsworth: Penguin Books, 1962.

Skelton, Robin. *The Memoirs of a Literary Blockhead.* Toronto: Macmillan of Canada, 1988.

Smith, Warren S. *Bernard Shaw's Plays. ('Major Barbara,' 'Heartbreak House,' 'Saint Joan,' 'Too True To Be Good' With Backgrounds and Criticism).* New York: W.H. Norton & Co., 1970.

Strindberg, August. *Six Plays Of Strindberg.* Trans. Elizabeth Sprigge. Garden City, N.Y.: Doubleday Anchor, 1955.

Stuart, E. Ross. *The History of Prairie Theatre. (The Development of Theatre In Alberta, Manitoba and Saskatchewan 1833-1982).* Toronto: Simon & Pierre, 1984.

Trewin, J.C. *The Edwardian Theatre.* Oxford: Basil Blackwell, 1976.

Tynan, Kenneth. *A View of the English Stage.* Frogmore, St. Albans, Herts: Paladin, 1976.

Valency, Maurice. *The Cart and the Trumpet. (The Plays of George Bernard Shaw).* New York: Schocken Books, 1983.

Weintraub, Stanley, ed. *The Portable Bernard Shaw.* Harmondsworth: Penguin Books, 1982.

West, E.H., ed. *Shaw On Theatre.* New York: Hill and Wang, 1965.

Woodbridge, Homer E. *G.B. Shaw: Creative Artist.* Carbondale: Southern Illinois University Press, 1965.

Young, Stark. *Immortal Shadows. (A Book of Dramatic Criticism).* New York: Hill and Wang, 1948.

APPENDIX

1980

MISALLIANCE at the Festival Theatre, May 28-October 5 (68 perfs.)

Johnny Tarleton	Peter Hutt
Bentley Summerhays	James Rankin
Hypatia Tarleton	Deborah Kipp
Mrs. Tarleton	Marion Gilsenan
Lord Summerhays	David Dodimead
John Tarleton Sr.	Sandy Webster
Joseph Percival	Geraint Wyn Davies
Lina Szczepanowska	Carole Shelley
Julius Baker ("Gunner")	Andrew Gillies

Directed by Christopher Newton
Designed by Cameron Porteous
Lighting by Jeffrey Dallas
(Archival tape was of a performance on August 21, 1980)

1981

SAINT JOAN at the Festival Theatre, May 27-October 4, (69 perfs.)

Robert de Baudricourt	William Webster
The Steward	Al Kozlik
Joan	Nora McLellan
Bertrand de Poulengy	Stephen Ouimette
Archbishop of Rheims	Jack Medley
Duc de la Tremouille	Richard Farrell
Page to Charles VII	Dan Lett
Gilles de Rais	James Rankin
Captain La Hire	John Lefebvre
The Dauphin, Charles VII	Heath Lamberts
Duchesse de la Tremouille	Dianne Sokoluk
Dunois	Peter Dvorsky
Page to Dunois	Duncan McIntosh
Earl of Warwick	Robert Benson
John de Stogumber	Barry MacGregor
Peter Cauchon	David Hemblen
Page to Warwick	Paul Eves
Sergeant at Arms	Andrew Lewarne
The Inquisitor	Herb Foster
Brother Martin	Tom McCamus
D'Estivet	Stephen Ouimette
De Courcelles	William Webster
Executioner	Keith James
English Soldier	Richard Farrell
English Gentleman	John Lefebvre
Duc de Vendome	Peter Krantz
Ladies in Waiting	Elizabeth Christmas, Dianne Sokoluk
Page/Monk	Andrew Lewarne

Directed by Christopher Newton
Designed by Cameron Porteous
Lighting by Jeffrey Dallas
Music by Allan Rae
(Archival tape of a performance on August 28, 1981)

1983

CAESAR AND CLEOPATRA at the Festival Theatre, May 25-October 1 (62 perfs.)

Caesar	Douglas Rain
Cleopatra	Marti Maraden
Nubian Slave/Courtier	David Collins
Ftatateeta	Diane Douglass
Charmian	Susan Stackhouse
Iras	Brigit Wilson
Harpist/Courtier	Tracy Bell
Rufio	David Hemblen
Centurion	Christopher Thomas
Roman Soldier/Porter	Richard Rebiere
Roman Soldier	Peter Keleghan
Roman Soldier/Court Official	Dan Lett
Roman Soldier	Carl Marotte
Roman Soldier	Craig Walker
Sentinel	Stuart Hughes
Courtier/Votary	Leonard Chow
Pothinus	Robert Benson
Ptolemy/Courtier	Duncan McIntosh
Theodotus	Al Kozlik
Achillas	David Schurmann
Brittanus	Herb Foster
Lucius Septimius	Rodger Barton
Apollodorus	Geoffrey Bowes
Courtier/First Porter	Ken McAuliffe
Boatman/Courtier	Keith Knight
Musician/Porter	Andrew Lewarne
Major Domo	John Gilbert
Bel Affris	Peter Krantz
The Persian	Tom McCamus
Belzanor	Hugo Dann

Directed by Christopher Newton
Designed by Cameron Porteous
Lighting by Jeffrey Dallas
Fight staged by Peter Krantz
(Archival Tape of a performance on August 28, 1983)

1985

HEARTBREAK HOUSE at the Festival Theatre, May 22-October 5 (63 perfs.)

Ellie Dunn	Marti Maraden
Nurse Guinness	Jennifer Phipps
Captain Shotover	Douglas Rain
Ariadne (Lady Utterword)	Fiona Reid
Hesione Hushabye	Goldie Semple
Mazzini Dunn	Allan Gray
Hector Hushabye	Norman Browning
Boss Mangan	Robert Benson
Randall Utterword	Peter Krantz
Burglar	Andrew Gillies
Gardener's Boys	Jim Jones, Ric Sarabia

Directed by Christopher Newton
Designed by Michael Levine
Lighting by Jeffrey Dallas
(Archival tape of a performance on June 1, 1985)

1987

MAJOR BARBARA at the Festival Theatre, May 27-October 11 (73 perfs.)

Lady Britomart Undershaft	Frances Hyland
Stephen Undershaft	Steven Sutcliffe
Morrison	Al Kozlik
Barbara Undershaft	Martha Burns
Sarah Undershaft	Barbara Worthy
Adolphus Cusins	Jim Mezon
Charles Lomax	Michael Howell
Andrew Undershaft	Douglas Rain
Rummy Mitchens	Irene Hogan
Snobby Price	Ted Dykstra
Peter Shirley	Herb Foster
Jenny Hill	Helen Taylor
Bill Walker	Jon Bryden
Mrs. Baines	Jennifer Phipps

| Salvation Army Worker | Grant Carmichael |
| Bilton | Al Kozlik |

Directed by Christopher Newton
Designed by Cameron Porteous
Lighting by Jeffrey Dallas
Music arrangement by Roger Perkins
Sound designed by Walter Lawrence
(Archival tape of a dress rehearsal on May 5, 1987)

1988

YOU NEVER CAN TELL at the Festival Theatre, May 25-October 15 (79 perfs.)

Also played at the Manitoba Theatre Centre, Winnipeg, January 27-February 20, Olympic Arts Festival, Calgary, February 23-27, and Theatre Calgary, March 1-20 with Frances Hyland in the role of Mrs. Clandon.

Dolly	Helen Taylor
Mr. Valentine	Andrew Gillies
Parlormaid	Jane Wheeler
Philip	Steven Sutcliffe
Mrs. Clandon	Barbara Gordon
Gloria	Mary Haney
Mr. Crampton	Sandy Webster
M'Comas	Robert Benson
The Waiter	Douglas Rain
Bohun	Craig Davidson
The Cook	Patric Masurkevitch
Jo (a Waiter)	Lance McDayter
Waiter	Mark Burgess

Directed by Christopher Newton
Designed by Cameron Porteous
Lighting by Robert Thomson
Original Music composed by Christopher Donison
(Archival tape of a performance at Theatre Calgary)

1989

MAN AND SUPERMAN at the Festival Theatre, May 24-October 15 (including DON JUAN IN HELL) (79 perfs.)

Roebuck Ramsden	William Hutt
Octavius Robinson	Peter Krantz
Parlormaid	Monica Dufault
John Tanner	Michael Ball
Ann Whitefield	Kate Trotter
Mrs. Whitefield	Jennifer Phipps
Miss Ramsden	Marion Gilsenan
Violet Robinson	Julie Stewart
Henry Straker	William Vickers
Hector Malone	Patric Masurkevitch
Mr. Malone	Al Kozlik
Mendoza	Barry MacGregor
The Anarchist	Robert Haley
The English Socialist	Peter Windrem
The German Socialist	Dean Cooney
Duval	Tom Wood
Sulky Social Democrat	Richard Waugh
Rowdy Social Democrat	Blair Williams
Goatherd	Callum Rennie
A Spanish Officer	Dean Cooney
Singer	Gail Hakala
Pianist	Christopher Donison

the *DON JUAN IN HELL* scene was added to Act III for 13 perfs.

Don Juan Tenorio	Michael Ball
Dona Ana de Ulloa	Kate Trotter
Commander of Calatrava (The Statue)	William Hutt
The Devil	Barry MacGregor
Satanic Guests	Dean Cooney, Robert Haley, Callum Rennie, Ric Waugh, Blair Williams, Peter Windrem, Tom Wood

Directed by Christopher Newton
Designed by Eduard Kochergin
Lighting by Robert Thomson
Music composed by Christopher Donison
Sound designed by Walter Lawrence
(Archival tape of a performance on July 18, 1989)

1990

MISALLIANCE at the Festival Theatre, May 23-October 14 (87 perfs.)

The Maid	Michelle Cecile Martin
The Gardener	Bart Anderson
Jock	Murray Oliver
Bill Burt	Neil Barclay
Bentley Summerhays	Duncan Ollerenshaw
Johnny Tartleton	Mark Burgess
Hypatia Tarleton	Helen Taylor
Mrs. Tarleton	Jennifer Phipps
Lord Summerhays	Richard Farrell
Mr. Tarleton	Barry MacGregor
Joey Percival	Peter Krantz
Lina Szczepanowska	Sharry Flett
Gunner (Julius Baker)	Simon Bradbury

Directed by Christopher Newton
Designed by Leslie Frankish
Lighting by Robert Thomson
Sound design by Walter Lawrence
(Archival tape of a performance on May 20, 1990)

Index of Names